MICRO FACTS!

500 FANTASTIC FACTS about
SPACE

ANNE ROONEY

ARCTURUS

ARCTURUS

This edition published in 2019 by Arcturus Publishing Limited
26/27 Bickels Yard, 151–153 Bermondsey Street,
London SE1 3HA

ISBN: 978-1-78950-660-0
CH005760NT
Supplier 29, Date 0419, Print run 6990

Author: Anne Rooney
Designer: Sarah Fountain
Editor: Joe Harris
Illustrators: Jake McDonald and Señor Sanchez
Supplementary artworks: Shutterstock

Printed in China

CONTENTS

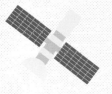

THE FIRST OBJECT IN SPACE LOOKED LIKE A SPIKY BASKETBALL

The satellite was Sputnik, launched October 4, 1957 from the USSR. It was a shiny metal ball just 58 cm (23 in) across with four long radio antennae.

Sputnik was blasted into orbit around the Earth, where it whizzed round at 29,000 km/h (18,000 mph). It made 1,440 orbits, each taking just 96.2 minutes, before burning up re-entering Earth's atmosphere on January 4, 1958.

For three weeks, Sputnik transmitted beeps that could be picked up even by amateur radio enthusiasts. It stopped transmitting when its batteries ran out.

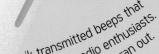

4

WILL.I.AM HAS SUNG ON MARS

The first music ever broadcast from another planet was a song by the American singer and rapper Will.i.am of the Black Eyed Peas.

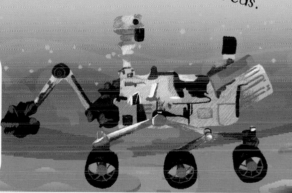

NASA's Curiosity rover broadcast the song back to Earth, but didn't take speakers—so if there is any life on Mars, it didn't get to hear it.

US astronauts Walter Schirra and Thomas P. Stafford were the first people to play musical instruments in space. They played "Jingle Bells" on an eight-note harmonica and some bells while orbiting Earth on Gemini 6A in 1965. They pretended to be a UFO called Santa Claus.

VOYAGER 1
AND VOYAGER 2
are the only spacecraft that have left our solar system.

The Voyagers will carry on going at 48,280 km/h (30,000 mph) forever unless they are destroyed in a collision.

Both Voyagers were launched in 1977. Voyager 1 is now 21 billion km (13 billion miles) away.

Voyager 1 is so far from the Sun that it takes 18 hours for sunlight to reach it. The spacecraft travels at 17 km (11 miles) per second.

The Voyagers' instruments will send back data to Earth until around 2030, when their power supplies will fail.

The Voyagers could never leave the galaxy, even in billions of years, because they're too slow to escape its gravity

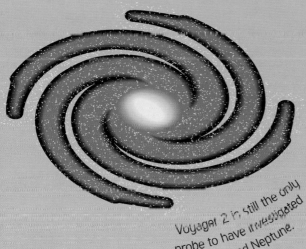

Voyager 2 is still the only probe to have investigated Uranus and Neptune.

The Voyagers are in daily contact with Earth. A radio message now takes 18 hours to get here.

Each Voyager carries a Golden Record holding sounds and photos from Earth and showing where Earth is in the solar system and galaxy.

It will be 40,000 years before either Voyager comes even slightly close to another star.

THE SPEECH WAS WRITTEN
IN ADVANCE FOR AN APOLLO DISASTER

The Apollo 11 Moon landing was a daring
and dangerous mission, and the eyes of the world
were on the three astronauts.

What if it went wrong? What if they could not get off
the Moon? The US President Richard Nixon had his
speech written in advance, just in case:

"These brave men, Neil Armstrong and
Edwin Aldrin, know that there is no hope for
their recovery. But they also know that there
is hope for mankind in their sacrifice."

... but of course the mission was a success.

IN SPACE, COFFEE CRAWLS OUT OF THE CUP

In zero gravity, in a spaceship, liquids don't stay where they are put. They crawl up the side of a cup or out of the top of a bottle and fly around in the air.

To drink, astronauts can suck liquid from a pouch, or use a specially designed cup that uses capillary action—the liquid sticks to the walls of the container and is naturally drawn upward. You can see capillary action work if you put a sponge in a bowl of water—the liquid goes upward into the sponge.

ASTRONAUTS on the International Space Station 3D-PRINT TOOLS THEY NEED

Since 2014, the International Space Station (ISS) has had a 3D printer so that crew can make tools or spare parts they need.

Space launches are expensive, so taking material that can be turned into tools when needed makes more sense than taking lots of tools that might never be used.

A "refabricator" recycles printed items. A tool can be printed, used, then melted down and printed into something else.

SERGEI VOLKOV is the only SECOND-GENERATION SPACE EXPLORER

The Russian cosmonaut Sergei Volkov has spent more than a year in space, split between two missions to the ISS.

His father, Aleksandr, was also a cosmonaut, visiting two earlier space stations, Salyut and Mir. Sergei is the only second-generation cosmonaut or astronaut in the world.

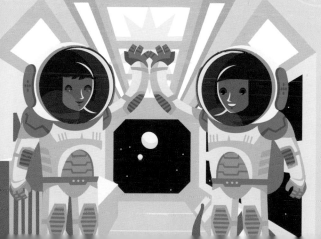

Identical twins Scott and Mark Kelly both visited the International Space Station at the same in time 2011. Scott was part of a Russian mission, and Mark flew with the US shuttle Endeavor.

AMERICAN SPACECRAFT LAND IN WATER, RUSSIAN SPACECRAFT ON LAND

The part of a spacecraft that carries astronauts back to Earth needs to land safely.

Landing in the sea is fairly safe, besides the risk of drowning. American spacecraft take off over sea (so that they can abort safely in an emergency) and splashdown into the sea. But then, America has a lot of reasonably warm sea nearby.

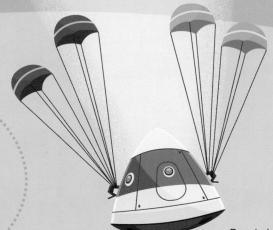

Russia has much less coast, and what it has is in the polar north, so it is not a good place to land. So Russian craft come down in areas of empty land. Russia has a lot of that.

Venus was once thought to be a LUSH WORLD OF TROPICAL JUNGLE

Venus is closer to the Sun than Earth, so it seems reasonable that it will be warmer.

Until the 1960s, people imagined either a world covered by a warm ocean with maybe a few islands, or a swampy planet inhabited by strange, exotic animals and plants.

When the USSR sent the Venera probes to explore Venus, they were designed to land in water. In 1967, Venera 4 even had a lock made of sugar that would dissolve on contact with water to release an extra communications antenna. Now, though, we know its surface is rocky— and there are only traces of water.

Pioneer 10 will take TWO MILLION YEARS TO REACH THE NEXT STAR

The Pioneer 10 spacecraft, launched in 1972, was the first to fly past Jupiter in 1973. It then headed for the edge of the solar system.

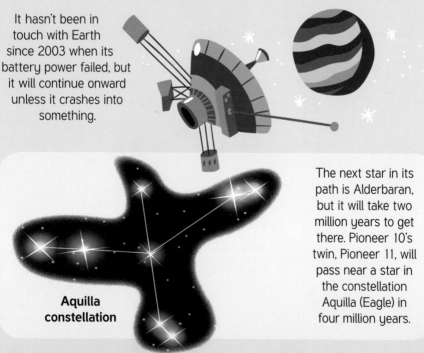

It hasn't been in touch with Earth since 2003 when its battery power failed, but it will continue onward unless it crashes into something.

The next star in its path is Alderbaran, but it will take two million years to get there. Pioneer 10's twin, Pioneer 11, will pass near a star in the constellation Aquilla (Eagle) in four million years.

Aquilla constellation

THE FIRST HUMAN IN SPACE DIDN'T EXPECT TO SURVIVE

The first human being in space was the Russian Yuri Gagarin on April 12, 1961.

He spent just 108 minutes in space as pilot of the Soviet spacecraft Vostok 1.

Gagarin didn't tell his mother he was going because the mission was top secret.

And he didn't tell his wife the true date of his flight, but instead told her a later date (by which time he was home). Just in case, he left her a letter saying he didn't expect to return and she should remarry if he died.

15

TO TRAP SPACEDUST, NASA USED ALMOST INVISIBLE "AEROGEL"

A mission called Stardust collected tiny pieces of space rock from outside our solar system, trapping them in a super-light gel.

Aerogel

Spacedust moves six times as fast as a rifle bullet. NASA needed a way of trapping the bits without breaking them. Aerogel is solid, but 99.8% air and doesn't harm the particles.

No one knew how to get the particles back out of the aerogel or even started thinking about it until four years after Stardust's launch. The samples came back in 2014, but it will take years to investigate the tiny specks.

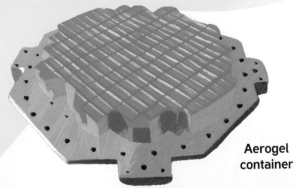

Aerogel container

"EAT ME" MESSAGES
might lead aliens to us

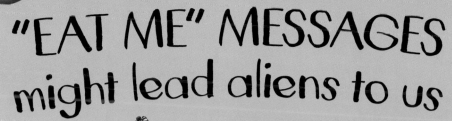

Two pairs of spacecraft, Voyagers 1 and 2 and Pioneers 10 and 11, are both heading out of the solar system into interstellar space carrying messages for any aliens that might find them.

Both Pioneers have a metal plaque on the outside showing two adult humans and a map of where Earth is.

Some people think this is a bad idea, amounting to advertising ourselves as a snack on a planet that could be raided for resources. Let's hope they're wrong!

YOU CAN'T GO IN A STRAIGHT LINE TO MARS

When spacecraft go to Mars, they loop around the Sun in a curved path that meets up with Mars.

Earth and Mars orbit the Sun at different speeds. The best time to leave for Mars is calculated from the positions and speeds of both planets. Mars must be in the right place when the spacecraft's orbit intersects the orbit of Mars.

Depart Earth
September 2022

Depart Mars
July 2024

Arrive Earth
March 2025

Arrive Mars
April 2023

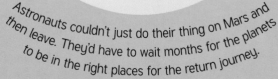

Astronauts couldn't just do their thing on Mars and then leave. They'd have to wait months for the planets to be in the right places for the return journey.

SOON, WE WILL HEAR FROM MARS

A rover due to land on Mars in 2021 is going to have microphones so that it can send back to Earth the sounds of its own landing and travel across the surface of the planet. We'll be able to hear its wheels crunching over Martian stones.

It will also have clever cameras for taking different types of photo—including for photographing itself, as what kind of rover would want to go to Mars and not take selfies?

The new rover will have a nuclear battery that can keep it running for ten years.

PLANETARY ROVERS CAN LOWER THEMSELVES TO THE SURFACE WITH A CRANE

—which is pretty clever when there is nothing on the surface yet. The rover uses a special "sky crane" which it carries with it.

It looks like a puppet being lowered by a flying puppeteer.

The rover and crane use a parachute to come down through the planet's atmosphere, firing rockets toward the surface to slow them down. Then the crane gently lowers the lander by a cable to the surface.

The crane has a bad ending, though. It cuts the cables, flies away, and crashes into the planet's surface.

A SATELLITE "LOST IN SPACE" WAS FOUND AFTER SEVEN YEARS

The first Indian spacecraft to go to the Moon, Chandrayaan-1, went missing in 2009 when it stopped broadcasting signals back to Earth.

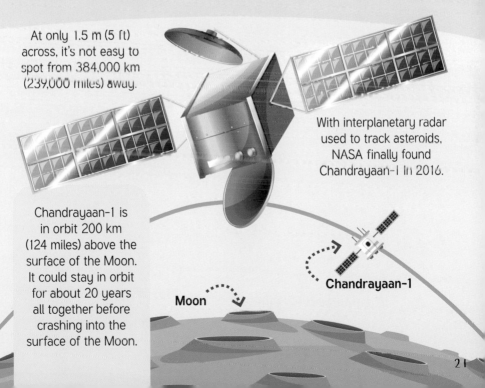

At only 1.5 m (5 ft) across, it's not easy to spot from 384,000 km (239,000 miles) away.

With interplanetary radar used to track asteroids, NASA finally found Chandrayaan-1 in 2016.

Chandrayaan-1 is in orbit 200 km (124 miles) above the surface of the Moon. It could stay in orbit for about 20 years all together before crashing into the surface of the Moon.

Moon

Chandrayaan-1

A JAPANESE SPACECRAFT CARRIED A BIT OF AN ASTEROID TO AUSTRALIA

Hayabusa landed for 30 minutes on an asteroid called 25143 Itokawa in 2005.

It scooped up a tiny sample of the surface—just a few grains—and returned it to Earth, dropping it in a capsule with a parachute to land in Australia in 2010.

Hayabusa also carried a miniature lander, just 10 cm (3.9 in) by 12 cm (4.7 in), that was designed to hop across the surface taking photos. It was released but missed the asteroid, drifting off into space instead.

YOU COULD TELL NASA'S JUNOCAM WHAT TO DO

NASA's Juno mission to Jupiter has a camera, JunoCam, which regularly sends back images to Earth. They are available to anyone in the world.

People can suggest features of Jupiter for JunoCam to focus on, and can vote on suggestions. In this way, NASA crowdsources plans for Juno.

LOTS OF OLD SPACECRAFT ARE STUCK IN ORBIT AROUND THE SUN

When spacecraft are sent to somewhere and don't get there, they don't just disappear—they end up going around the Sun.

At least 65 spacecraft and bits of spacecraft are currently going around and around the Sun.

They include old probes that have done their job (or got lost on the way), satellites that are still working hard and also lots of smaller parts, such as sections and panels dropped by rockets going to the Moon.

Even the junk could keep going round for millions or billions of years.

24

THERE IS A CAR IN ORBIT AROUND THE SUN

In 2018, American businessman Elon Musk launched a red Tesla Roadster into space as a test load for the new Falcon Heavy rocket.

Before blasting it to space, Musk had used the electric sports car to commute in Los Angeles, USA.

It's "driven" by a dummy in a spacesuit. A plaque on the engine reads "Made on Earth by humans."

The car will reach a maximum speed of 121,600 km/h (75,600 mph). Parts of it could last for billions of years, but in a few hundred million years its orbit will change. It might dive into the Sun or be thrown out of the solar system.

DUST CAN PUNCH STRAIGHT THROUGH A SPACESHIP

Micrometeors are tiny particles, just a fraction of an inch across. Although they're tiny, they can do serious damage as they slam into spacecraft at huge speeds.

Spacecraft and satellites need a bullet-proof coat to protect them. Often, this is a layer of light metal over a layer of Kevlar, on top of the spacecraft's outer shell.

A micrometeor is usually smashed to dust on the outer metal, and the force of the impact is spread out by the protective coat.

NASA'S FIRST MERCURY ROCKET FLEW TO ONLY 10 CM (4 IN)

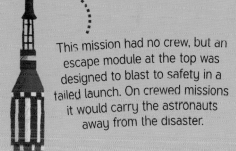

The Redstone-Mercury rocket, launched in 1960, was the first attempt to launch a spacecraft that could carry a probe to Mercury.

This mission had no crew, but an escape module at the top was designed to blast to safety in a failed launch. On crewed missions it would carry the astronauts away from the disaster.

The rocket rose only 10 cm (4 in) before its engines cut off and it settled back onto the launch pad. The escape rocket then fired and rose to a height of 1,200 m (4,000 ft) and landed 370 m (400 yd) away.

Engineers considered shooting the fuel tanks with a rifle to release pressure and prevent an explosion. They decided against this risky course of action and instead just waited for the battery to run out.

ASTEROIDS MIGHT BE DRAGGED THROUGH SPACE AND MINED FOR THEIR CONTENTS

A company based in California and Belgium intends to start mining asteroids for valuable metals and minerals.

It's designing a spacecraft that will capture asteroids and drag them through space to a space station (not yet built) for processing.

They hope their space station will become a layover for craft journeying between planets to stock up on fuel, oxygen, water, and other useful supplies.

THE FIRST WOMAN IN SPACE
didn't tell her mother she was going

The Russian cosmonaut Valentina Tereshkova became the first woman in space in 1963, with a three-day trip on Vostok 6.

Tereshkova's mother found out about her daughter's trip only when she saw the latest pictures from space on television. Although the picture was grainy, it was obvious to her that it was Valentina. She knew her daughter had taken parachute training—but that's all!

THE MOST ADVENTUROUS ROVER IS OPPORTUNITY

Rovers travel over the surface of other planets and the Moon, but they don't go very far.

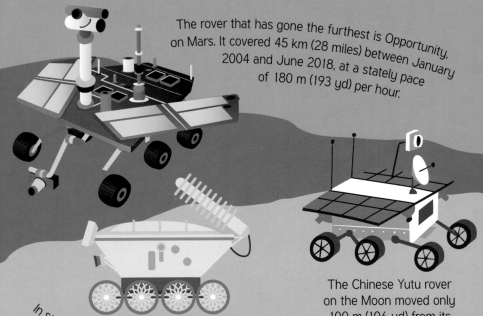

The rover that has gone the furthest is Opportunity, on Mars. It covered 45 km (28 miles) between January 2004 and June 2018, at a stately pace of 180 m (193 yd) per hour.

The Chinese Yutu rover on the Moon moved only 100 m (106 yd) from its landing site.

In second place is the Soviet Lunokohd 2, which journeyed 36.4 km (22.6 miles) across the Moon in 1973.

A NEW PROBE WILL BLOW GAS AT AN ASTEROID

The probe OSIRIS-REx, launched in 2016, reached the asteroid Bennu in 2018 and will map its surface for two years.

Then it will blow puffs of nitrogen gas at the asteroid to dislodge bits of it.

OSIRIS-REx will try to catch at least 60 g (2 oz) of material, then bring it back to Earth in 2023.

It will drop the capsule with the samples and go into orbit around the Sun forever.

MOST OF A SPACE ROCKET IS THROWN AWAY IN THE FIRST FEW MINUTES

It takes a huge amount of energy to blast a rocket into space. It gets the energy from burning fuel.

Rockets are designed in stages, with whole chunks used for just the first part of the journey, carrying fuel.

That means they can be dropped as soon as the rocket has used the fuel.

The Saturn V rocket used to launch the Apollo missions dropped two stages—most of the rocket—in the first 12 minutes, and another within three hours.

NASA WILL SEND AN "ICE MOLE" TO LOOK FOR LIFE IN THE OCEANS OF ENCELADUS

The ocean beneath the frozen surface of Saturn's moon Enceladus is one of the most likely places to find life beyond Earth.

NASA plans a mission to Enceladus, using a probe called IceMole to melt through some of the ice and take samples. It's already been used to bore through ice in Antarctica.

IceMole can look after itself, choosing a route through the ice and avoiding any obstacles it comes across.

It's not looking for large undersea creatures—maybe tiny microbes at the best. But who knows?

33

A video games designer
OWNS A LANDER ON THE MOON

Richard Garriott bought the Soviet Luna 21 and its Lunokhod 2 rover in 1993 for US$68,500—but they are both still on the Moon.

The craft were sent to the Moon in 1973. Lunokhod 2 journeyed 36.4 km (22.6 miles) over the Moon's surface before being disabled by dust. It is still used for bouncing lasers off to measure the distance to the Moon (see page 130).

Garriott claims that he owns the area of the Moon occupied by his craft.

Lunokhod 2 ·······>

More than 200,000 people applied to go to Mars—AND NEVER COME BACK

By far the hardest part of a trip to Mars is taking off for the return journey. Staying there avoids that problem. When the Mars One Foundation asked for volunteers for a one-way trip lots of people wanted to go.

It wouldn't necessarily be lonely for long. Every 26 months, Earth and Mars are in the right places for another spaceship to fly out, potentially taking more people.

One space scientist has suggested just one person would go, or maybe a couple.

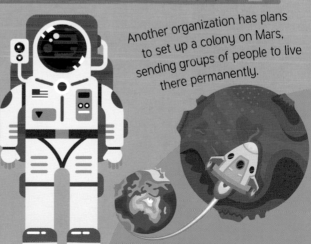

Another organization has plans to set up a colony on Mars, sending groups of people to live there permanently.

35

GOING INTO **SPACE** ISN'T GOOD FOR YOU

Space can have some strange effects on the human body.

The heart shrinks without gravity as it has less work to do pumping blood around the body.

Identical twins Scott and Mark Kelly have been studied by NASA: Scott spent a year on the ISS while Mark stayed on Earth and their health was compared.

People grow taller in space without gravity dragging them down. After a year in space, Scott Kelly grew 5 cm (2 in).

Bones weaken, as they don't have to work hard without gravity.

If you cry in space, the tears don't fall—they clump together into a big ball that eventually floats away.

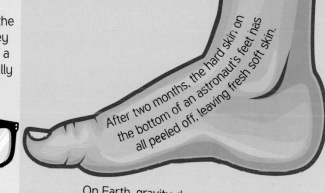

After two months, the hard skin on the bottom of an astronaut's feet has all peeled off, leaving fresh soft skin.

Eyesight deteriorates, so astronauts who wear glasses often need stronger ones after a few months in space.

On Earth, gravity drags fluid down the body, but in space there's more at the top of the body. It can cause a puffy face and headaches.

Astronauts' muscles waste away unless they do lots of exercise—at least two hours a day.

Some astronauts lose their sense of taste or their tastes change so that they like things they don't usually like or dislike things they usually like.

It takes 5-10 months to get to Mars and astronauts will be away for 2-3 years, cooped up in a small space with other people. It will be emotionally and mentally hard as well as physically demanding.

NASA PLANS A LUNAR OUTPOST AS A GATEWAY TO SPACE

NASA's base in space will sit between Earth and the Moon, and will support expeditions to the Moon and to Mars.

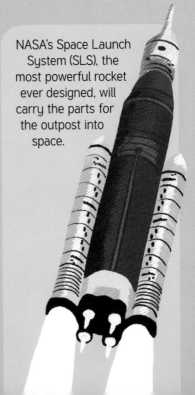

NASA's Space Launch System (SLS), the most powerful rocket ever designed, will carry the parts for the outpost into space.

A solar-powered "power and propulsion" unit should be launched in 2022, and somewhere for astronauts to live will follow in 2023.

SPIDERS IN SPACE BECAME CELEBRITIES

NASA sent two golden orb spiders to the ISS for 45 days in 2011. They were called Gladys and Esmeralda.

More than 130,000 students signed up to follow the investigation into how well they could spin webs in microgravity (Pretty well, as it turned out.)

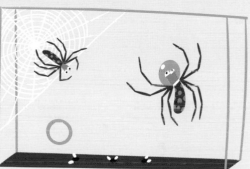

An earlier attempt at the experiment was given up after eight days.

The spiders eat fruit flies, and astronauts released all the fruit flies into the spider habitat immediately. Soon, fruit-fly smear covered the glass, making it impossible to see what was happening inside the spider habitat.

A GERMAN RAN THE AMERICAN SPACE PROGRAM

At the end of the Second World War, many German scientists surrendered to the USA.

Among them was rocket scientist Wernher von Braun and his research team. He was taken to America, where he eventually became the first director of NASA.

Von Braun proposed a space station, planned a trip to Mars, and designed the Saturn V rockets that took the Apollo craft into space.

He had designed the German Army's V2 rocket, and based the design for the Saturn V on it.

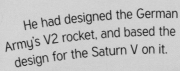

TIME GOES MORE SLOWLY on the ISS than on Earth

Astronauts age more slowly than people stuck on Earth—but only very slightly.

An astronaut on the International Space Station (ISS) gains just one hundredth of a second a year.

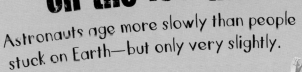

Time goes more slowly closer to a massive object, like a planet, so it should be slower on Earth than on the ISS.

But time also goes more slowly at high speeds. The ISS moves fast enough to make up for being in space and still get an advantage.

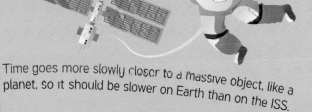

If an astronaut hung around in space without moving, they would age more quickly than on Earth—very slightly.

NO HUMAN HAS EVER FLOWN FASTER THAN THE CREW OF APOLLO 10

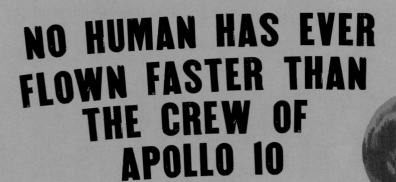

On the way back from orbiting the Moon in 1969, Apollo 10 reached 39,897 km/h (24,791 mph)—the fastest speed ever achieved by a vehicle carrying a crew.

The uncrewed robotic spacecraft Juno reached 266,000 km/h (165,000 mph) as it was pulled toward Jupiter by the planet's gravity in 2014. But the Parker Solar Probe, heading for the Sun, will have a top speed of 692,000 km/h (430,000 mph).

We care about
THE ALIENS

Every spacecraft carries some microbes from Earth into space.

These could contaminate a planet or moon that might have life of its own, possibly causing harm or changing the course of evolution.

Under an international agreement, all spacecraft are cleaned super-thoroughly to destroy any microbes. The target is to take no more than 300,000 microbes on any spacecraft.

The Juno spacecraft, sent to explore Jupiter and its moons, plunged into the huge gas giant at the end of its mission so that it couldn't ever crash into one of the moons that might have some form of life.

A town in Wyoming, USA, had a SPACEPORT FOR ALIENS FROM JUPITER

For around 20 years from 1994, the Wyoming town of Green River had the only spaceport set up to welcome refugees from Jupiter.

That year, NASA reported that Jupiter was in danger of being struck by broken chunks of comet.

GREATER GREEN RIVER INTERGALACTIC SPACEPORT

The residents of Green River worried for the creatures living on Jupiter (if there were any) and decided to welcome them.

It was the only official intergalactic space port in the world, but had only a windsock and a welcoming sign.

THE OBSERVATORY THAT FOUND PLUTO WAS BUILT TO INVESTIGATE MARTIANS

American businessman Percival Lowell built the Lowell Observatory in Flagstaff, Arizona, to explore the "canals" reported on Mars (see page 165) when Mars was close to Earth in 1896.

He was enthusiastic about the idea of intelligent life on Mars.

When the "canals" turned out not to exist, he turned his enthusiasm to looking for an extra planet.

He photographed Pluto in 1915, but as it was much fainter than he expected he didn't recognize it.

Pluto was officially discovered by Clyde Tombaugh in 1930, at Lowell's observatory.

ANIMALS IN SPACE

The first monkey to reach space was Albert II in 1949, but he died on the return journey.

A mouse survived going up into space in 1950, but the rocket fell apart coming back and it died.

Lots of different animals have been into space, including spiders, chicken embryos (in their eggs), newts, jellyfish, bees, and even Mexican jumping beans (there's a worm inside the bean).

The first living things sent into space were tiny fruit flies in 1947. They returned safely.

In 1959, two monkeys called Able and Baker survived a 16-minute flight and returned safely.

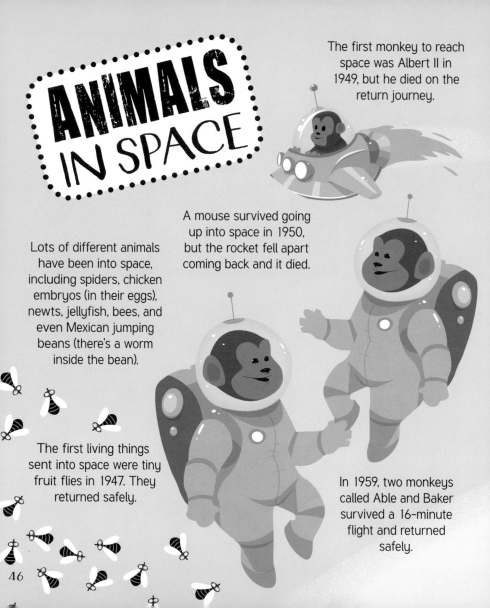

The most famous animal in space was a Russian stray dog, Laika, in 1957. She died on the flight.

Two Russian dogs, Veterok and Ugolyok, spent 22 days on Kosmos 110 in 1966, setting a record.

Two dogs, 42 mice, two rats, a rabbit, and a collection of fruit flies all went around the Earth on Sputnik 5 in 1960 and came back safely.

Zond 5 made the first orbit of the Moon in 1968, carrying two Russian tortoises, mealworms, wine flies, plants, seeds, and bacteria.

Water bears are tough microscopic creatures. They've survived being outside in outer space, where they're freezing cold, bombarded with radiation, and have no oxygen.

47

JELLYFISH BORN IN SPACE CAN'T COPE WITH GRAVITY

In the 1990s, astronauts bred more than 60,000 jellyfish on the Space Shuttle Columbia to investigate how they use gravity.

Jellyfish have a special organ to tell them which way up they are.

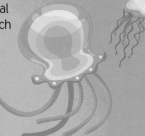

Tiny crystals roll around in a pocket lined with little hairs. The way that the hairs are disturbed tells the jellyfish which way is up and which way is down.

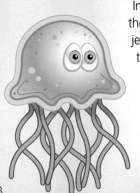

In the microgravity of space, there is no up or down, so the jellyfish never learn to "read" the movement of the hairs.

When they come back to Earth, their bodies can't understand gravity and they remain forever confused.

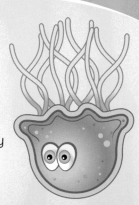

48

VENERA 7 SENT THE FIRST DATA from another planet

In 1970, the Soviet spacecraft arrived at the planet Venus—but it didn't get a soft landing.

Its parachute ripped and collapsed on the way through the acidic atmosphere, and Venera slammed into the scorching surface of Venus.

It sent back data on its way down, but then crashed and rolled over so that its antenna was not pointing toward Earth.

It seemed to go silent, but a week later scientists reviewing the tapes discovered it had carried on sending a weak signal for 23 minutes, gaining its place in the record books.

NASA'S VALKYRIE ROBOT WILL HELP BUILD ON MARS

Valkyrie (or R5) is a human-like robot, 1.9 m (6 ft 2 in) tall and weighing a hefty 136 kg (300 lb).

It can walk, see, use its hands—and put up with terrible working conditions.

It will work alongside astronauts on Mars, building shelters, mining for resources, and helping out with any problems.

The first humanoid robot in space was Robonaut 2.0, used on the International Space Station from 2012.

Robonaut originally had no legs, but has been given two "climbing manipulators." Robots in space are good for carrying out tasks that would be dangerous for humans.

COSMONAUT VALERI POLYAKOV holds the record for the LONGEST STAY IN SPACE

He spent nearly 438 days on Mir in a single visit in 1994-1995. That's more than a year and two months.

Russian Anatoly Solovyev has spent the longest time outside a spacecraft in space.

He's made 16 space walks, adding up to more than 82 hours and 10 minutes.

The person who has spent most time in space all together is cosmonaut Gennady Padalka, who has spent a total of 878 days in space over five missions on the ISS and the Russian space station Mir.

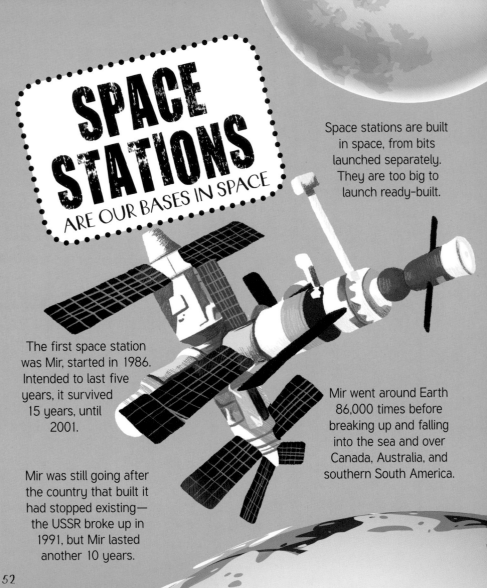

SPACE STATIONS
ARE OUR BASES IN SPACE

Space stations are built in space, from bits launched separately. They are too big to launch ready-built.

The first space station was Mir, started in 1986. Intended to last five years, it survived 15 years, until 2001.

Mir went around Earth 86,000 times before breaking up and falling into the sea and over Canada, Australia, and southern South America.

Mir was still going after the country that built it had stopped existing— the USSR broke up in 1991, but Mir lasted another 10 years.

The International Space Station (ISS) can be seen with the naked eye as a bright spot when it passes overhead. (Check **https://spotthestation.nasa.gov** to find out when you can see it.)

America's only space station, Skylab, was always called an "orbital workshop." NASA hoped to build a massive space station and didn't want anyone to think Skylab would do instead.

Forced to work 16-hour days, the last Skylab crew staged a small rebellion. They turned off the radio link with Earth and took a day off.

A 17-year-old Australian claimed a $10,000 prize offered by an American newspaper for finding part of Skylab. Chunks of the falling Skylab hit his house.

Although Skylab lasted five years, from 1974 to 1979, it had crew for only 171 days of that time.

EARTH IS THE ONLY ROCKY PLANET WITH FEW CRATERS

Mercury, Mars, and Venus are pitted with huge craters—so is the Moon—but Earth has very few. It's not because the Earth isn't hit by things, but because its surface "heals."

Wind, rain, moving ice, flowing floods, rivers, and the seas all wear away the surface of the Earth, so craters are soon smoothed out. But some are still visible.

The Vredefort crater in South Africa was 380 km (236 miles) across, when first created by a massive space rock 2 billion years ago.

It's about a third the size of Germany.

54

ROCKS FROM SPACE HIT EARTH ALL THE TIME

Meteors bombard Earth constantly, but most burn up in our atmosphere.

Big, small, and teeny tiny bits of rock collide with Earth every day, but as they whizz through the atmosphere they get so hot that they burn up completely.

If they are big enough, we see these burning meteors as shooting stars.

The bits that make it to Earth's surface are called meteorites. They're not all big lumps of rock or metal. Most are micrometeorites, so tiny you need a magnifying glass or microscope to see them.

THERE ARE MICROMETEORITES IN YOUR HOME

At less than a tenth of an inch across, micrometeorites don't fall fast enough to burn up in Earth's atmosphere and are small enough to get everywhere.

Micrometeorites blow or wash away easily, so we're not knee-deep in them. But they don't disappear—they build up, buried in Arctic snow, and sunk deep in the sea.

About 3 million kg (6.6 million lb) of micrometeorites land on Earth's surface every year. They're fairly evenly spread out—on average, one hits every 10,000 square cm (1 square yd) once a year. They're carried on air currents, even into your home and school.

THE SKY CAN BE GREEN— OR RED—OR VIOLET

The Northern and Southern lights are spectacular displays of swirling, changing shades of green, blue, yellow, red, and violet in the sky.

They're made by tiny charged particles streaming from the Sun and colliding with the gases of Earth's atmosphere.

They're only seen near the North and South poles because Earth's magnetic field pulls the particles toward Earth at the poles.

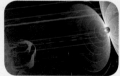

The patterns show up at both poles at the same time and are usually mirror images of each other. They can even be seen from above from space!

SPACE ROCKS CAN BE DEADLY

An asteroid that smashed into the Earth about 65 million years ago changed the conditions on the planet so much that many kinds of plants and animals died out— including most dinosaurs.

The crater made by the huge space rock was found in the Gulf of Mexico in 1978. The asteroid would have been 15 km (9.3 miles) across.

A substance called iridium, which is rare on Earth but common in asteroids, is found in rock layers around the world from 65 million years ago. This suggests tiny bits of the asteroid spread around the globe.

DAYS WERE SHORTER IN THE TIME OF THE DINOSAURS

When Earth first formed, it whizzed round on its axis, four or five times as fast as it does now, and days were just 5-6 hours long- or maybe even shorter.

Once the Moon formed (see page 104), the effort of dragging it around slowed the Earth's rotation and the days got longer.

My day was 22 minutes shorter than yours!

The Earth is still slowing down. In 100 years, a day will be two thousandths (0.02) of a second longer than it is now. That means that in 50,000 years, a day will be a whole second longer. It doesn't sound much—but over millions of years, it really adds up!

THE EARTH HAS LAYERS

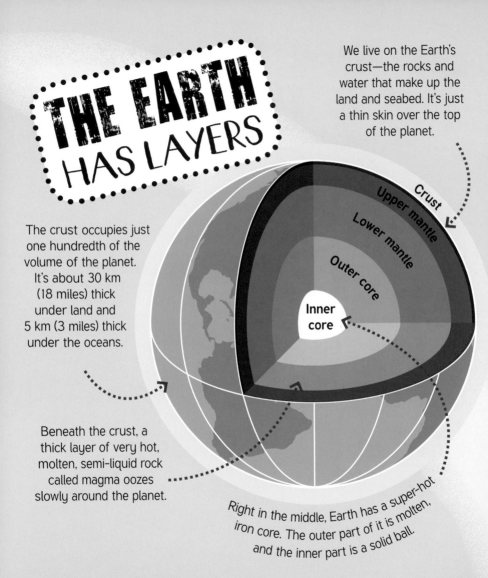

We live on the Earth's crust—the rocks and water that make up the land and seabed. It's just a thin skin over the top of the planet.

Crust

Upper mantle

Lower mantle

Outer core

Inner core

The crust occupies just one hundredth of the volume of the planet. It's about 30 km (18 miles) thick under land and 5 km (3 miles) thick under the oceans.

Beneath the crust, a thick layer of very hot, molten, semi-liquid rock called magma oozes slowly around the planet.

Right in the middle, Earth has a super-hot, iron core. The outer part of it is molten, and the inner part is a solid ball.

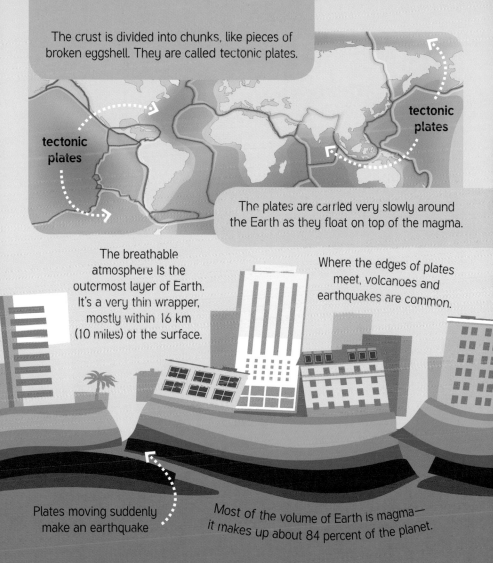

The crust is divided into chunks, like pieces of broken eggshell. They are called tectonic plates.

tectonic plates

tectonic plates

The plates are carried very slowly around the Earth as they float on top of the magma.

The breathable atmosphere is the outermost layer of Earth. It's a very thin wrapper, mostly within 16 km (10 miles) of the surface.

Where the edges of plates meet, volcanoes and earthquakes are common.

Plates moving suddenly make an earthquake

Most of the volume of Earth is magma—it makes up about 84 percent of the planet.

THE EARTH HAS A FAT MIDDLE

Earth isn't a true sphere—it's more like a ball that has been squashed from top and bottom, making the middle fatter than it should be and the Poles a bit flatter.

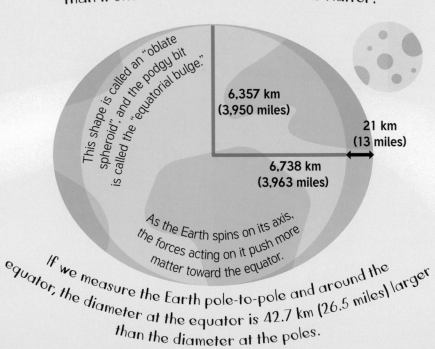

This shape is called an "oblate spheroid", and the podgy bit is called the "equatorial bulge."

6,357 km
(3,950 miles)

21 km
(13 miles)

6,738 km
(3,963 miles)

As the Earth spins on its axis, the forces acting on it push more matter toward the equator.

If we measure the Earth pole-to-pole and around the equator, the diameter at the equator is 42.7 km (26.5 miles) larger than the diameter at the poles.

ON THE MOON, EARTH HANGS IN ONE PLACE IN THE SKY

When we look up at the Moon, it seems to move across the sky from east to west during the night.

But that's because the Earth is rotating—your place on Earth moves in relation to the Moon as the Earth turns around. The same thing makes the Sun rise in the east and set in the west.

If you could stand on the Moon and look back at Earth, it wouldn't move across the sky.

The same side of the Moon always faces the Earth, so you would be looking straight at it all the time—unless you were on the wrong side, in which case you would never see Earth at all.

THE MOON WANDERS AROUND

The midline of the Earth—its fattest point—is called the equator. You might think the Moon would orbit Earth above the equator, but it doesn't stick to that path.

The Moon can stray up to 28.5 degrees above or below the equator over a month.

The Moon wandering about affects the tides (see page 129). Instead of all high and low tides being equal, some high tides are higher than others and some low tides lower than others.

When the Moon is straight above a bit of coast, that area will have higher tides than usual.

EARTH HAS A MICRO-"MOON"— but it only counts as an ASTEROID.

It's called 2016 HO3, which is not a very exciting name for a cosmic companion. It shares Earth's orbit around the Sun and seems to loop around Earth all the time, too.

It's about 38 times as far away as the Moon and is only 40–110 m (120–300 ft) across. It was spotted in 2016.

HO3 is called a "quasi-satellite." It's not close enough or permanent enough to count as a real moon.

Moon

Earth

HO3

It's been hanging around Earth for about 100 years, and will stay with us for several more centuries before drifting away.

IT'S COLDER AT THE POLES BECAUSE OF SLANTED SUNLIGHT

The rays that bring light and heat from the Sun strike Earth from straight above near the equator, but from a lower angle in the sky elsewhere.

At the poles, the same amount of sunlight is spread out over a greater area of land, so it has less heating effect.

Sun's rays

Most direct sunlight

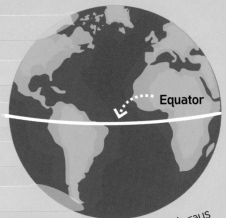

Equator

Between the poles and the equator, the Sun's rays come from somewhere between straight above and low on the horizon, so the temperature is in between very hot and very cold.

IT'S NOT EASY TO TELL THAT THE EARTH GOES AROUND THE SUN

Until about 1600, most people thought the Sun went around the Earth, though now we know the Earth goes around the Sun.

But what we see in the sky looks exactly the same either way— we can't tell which way it is without using mathematics.

People eventually worked out that the Earth moves around the Sun by making calculations and looking carefully at how the planets seem to move.

Sun · Mercury · Venus · Earth · Moon · Mars · Jupiter · Saturn

Ptolematic model of the Universe

Sun
Moon   Mars
Earth
          Mercury
Venus
  · Saturn   Jupiter

If the Sun and planets all moved around Earth, the planets would be doing a funny little backward-and-forward dance. But we couldn't absolutely prove what happens until we could go into space and look!

THE POLE STAR ISN'T ALWAYS AT THE POLE

In the northern part of the world, Polaris is the star closest to the celestial north pole (that's a line drawn from Earth's axis out into space). In the south, there is no pole star. At least, not just now...

The bit of sky directly above the poles changes, very slowly. That's because the Earth's axis wobbles, rather like a spinning top that is slowing down.

North celestial pole

Axis of rotation

It takes 25,700 years to make a full wobble. In 25,700 years, Polaris will be the pole star again.

South celestial pole

But there will be times in between when there is no pole star or a different star gets the starring role.

68

ALL EARTH'S OCEANS
might have come out of volcanoes

Earth is the only planet in the solar system with vast oceans of surface water, and it's not at all clear where all the water came from.

Scientists suggest four possible reasons for the world being so wet.

Perhaps water formed deep within the Earth and escaped from volcanoes.

Or maybe the bits of dust that gradually built up the Earth were already wet, so water was there from the start.

Even comets might have brought water to Earth.

Or asteroids and meteors carrying water crashed into Earth and spread it around.

EARTH GOES AROUND AND AROUND

It goes around on its own axis and it goes around the Sun. And then the Sun and the whole solar system go around the Milky Way.

Earth turns on its axis every 24 hours, making a day. It goes around the Sun every 365.25 days, making a year. (We collect up the quarter days and have an extra day in a leap year, every four years.)

What are you doing?

It's a leap year...

The whole solar system goes around the middle of the Milky Way, but that huge circle takes 230 million years to complete. Last time we were right where we are now, the dinosaurs were just getting started!

YOU'RE MOVING AT OVER HALF A MILLION MILES AN HOUR

If you stood still at the equator, just Earth's rotation on its axis would mean you'd be moving at 1,600 km/h (1,000 mph). You don't notice it because everything else is moving, too.

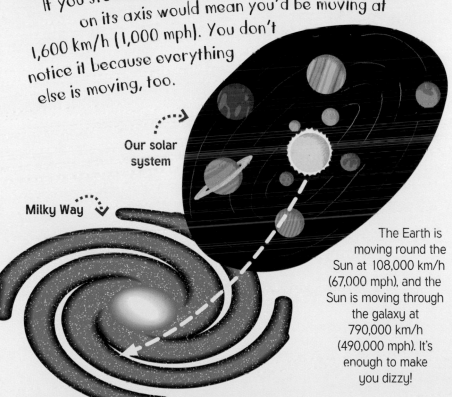

Our solar system

Milky Way

The Earth is moving round the Sun at 108,000 km/h (67,000 mph), and the Sun is moving through the galaxy at 790,000 km/h (490,000 mph). It's enough to make you dizzy!

SATELLITES ARE FALLING ALL THE TIME

Satellites are in orbit above the Earth all the time, but they're also constantly falling.

Satellites orbiting Earth are in free fall. This means they're being pulled toward Earth by gravity, but are moving just fast enough to avoid falling down to hit Earth. This works because the Earth is curved, and rotates.

Without gravity

With gravity

The satellite's speed is matched to the pull of gravity so that the satellite is kept suspended.

If it went too slowly, it would fall down. If it went too fast, it could whizz off into space.

72

SPACE JUNK IS A REAL PROBLEM

Just as there's too much trash on Earth, there's also too much of it in space.

Around half a million bits of "space junk" are tracked as they orbit Earth, moving at speeds of up to 27,350 km/h (17,500 mph). They could do real harm if they crashed into another satellite or a spacecraft, which is why they're tracked.

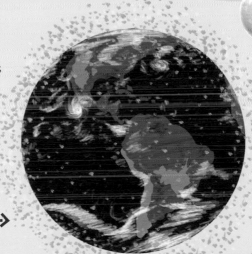

Most space junk is bits and pieces of old satellites that no longer work, and discarded parts of rockets that are dropped when no longer needed.

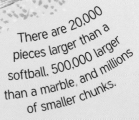

There are 20,000 pieces larger than a softball, 500,000 larger than a marble, and millions of smaller chunks.

SOME SCIENTISTS THINK LIFE ON EARTH CAME FROM SPACE

They're not suggesting huge lions, whales, or dinosaurs came from space, but tiny microbes, carried on comets or asteroids or just floating around in space.

Microbes from outer space could have landed on Earth, and Earth could have had just the right conditions for it to flourish—meaning life on Earth could have evolved from aliens!

The theory that life has been spread through the universe by comets and space dust is called "panspermia." It could explain life in many different star systems. So far, though, we haven't found any microbes on asteroids or comets.

WE HAVE SEASONS ONLY BECAUSE THE EARTH IS WONKY

Earth is tipped over in its orbit around the Sun. This means that the northern half of the world is tilted 23.5 degrees toward the Sun for part of the year, and the southern half for the opposite part of the year.

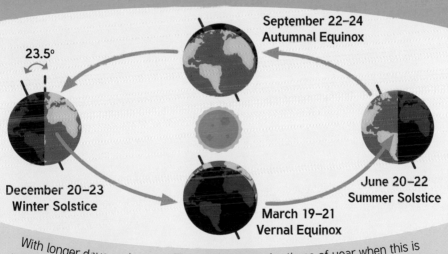

23.5°

September 22–24
Autumnal Equinox

December 20–23
Winter Solstice

March 19–21
Vernal Equinox

June 20–22
Summer Solstice

With longer days and more heat and light from the Sun, plants grow better in the summer.

The solstices are the times of year when this is most obvious—one end of the world has its shortest day and the other has its longest day. The equinoxes fall halfway between the solstices; days and nights are equal lengths at the equinox.

AIR MAKES THE SKY BLUE

Light from the Sun is white, but white light is made up of a whole rainbow of shades.

When the white light comes through Earth's atmosphere, the blue light in the spectrum is scattered more than the red, yellow, or green light—so the sky looks blue.

At sunset, the light from the Sun has passed through a lot of atmosphere by the time it reaches us and a lot of the blue light has been scattered away.

We see yellow light or, if there is dust in the atmosphere, red and orange. So sunsets come from a "dirty" sky.

Earth's atmosphere

SPACE RAYS COULD AFFECT YOUR PHONE

All our electronic gadgets, including phones and computers, use electromagnetic radiation to work. The Sun spends all day pouring out electromagnetic radiation into space—it's where our light and heat come from.

We've built our equipment to cope with the regular amount of background radiation from the Sun, but every now and then the Sun gets much more active and pours out great blasts of electromagnetic radiation. They won't fry all our electronics, but they can disrupt satellites, and even lead to power surges in the electricity network.

EARTH IS HEATED FROM THE INSIDE

The middle of the Earth is really hot—about 6,000 °C (10,800 °F). The heat comes from the decay of radioactive material and the leftover heat from the time Earth formed, 4,600 billion years ago.

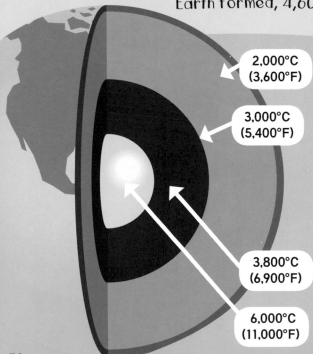

2,000°C
(3,600°F)

3,000°C
(5,400°F)

3,800°C
(6,900°F)

6,000°C
(11,000°F)

Earth's own heat has most impact underground. At the surface, it accounts for only 0.03 percent of Earth's heat energy, with all the rest coming from the Sun.

But you don't have to dig down far to find some heat. Just 5 km (3 miles) underground, the temperature is 170 °C (338 °F).

EARTH'S ATMOSPHERE MAKES A GOOD BLANKET—AND A GOOD SHIELD

Earth is kept a nice, even temperature by its atmosphere, which traps heat close to the surface.

Without it, a lot of heat would escape at night and heat would beat down on us during the day (except that we wouldn't be alive without the atmosphere, of course!).

Earth would be more like the Moon—scorching by day and freezing by night, varying by around 275 °C (500 °F).

The atmosphere doesn't just keep us cozy. It also saves us from being smashed by meteors. Most burn up in the atmosphere before they reach the ground, but without an atmosphere, Earth would be pitted with craters like the Moon.

SOMETIMES IT'S DARK ALL DAY
at the North and South Poles

The Earth is tilted on its axis at an angle of 23.5 degrees. That means the North Pole isn't really at the top and the South Pole isn't really at the bottom.

Earth

Night

Day

Sun

Equator

As a result, each pole is turned toward the Sun for part of the year and away from the Sun for part of the year. In December, the North Pole gets no light at all and in June, the South Pole gets no light.

While one pole gets no light, the other gets no night! The pole facing toward the Sun isn't fully turned away from it even at night-time.

How can it be bedtime? It's still light!

EARTH WAS ONCE A GIANT SNOWBALL

Or maybe more than once. Extreme climate change has happened several times in Earth's history.

About 700–600 million years ago, the whole of Earth's surface was covered with ice and the average temperature was just −50 °C (−58 °F).

The early life forms skulked deep in the oceans to keep going.

Once the surface was all white, it reflected back all the heat from the Sun and so it couldn't warm up again. It could have gone on forever, but Earth's volcanoes came to the rescue. They poured out carbon dioxide that trapped heat and slowly warmed the Earth again.

ALIENS LOOKING AT EARTH COULD MAYBE TELL WE'RE HERE

If they were close enough, they might notice radio waves that have leaked out into space over the last 100 years.

If they got close enough, they could see lights at night and pollution.

They could spot chemicals in our atmosphere that are a sign of life.

If they investigated the Moon or Mars, aliens might spot our abandoned spacecraft.

If they are more than 100 light years away, none of our radio signals will have reached them.

All the satellites and space junk orbiting Earth and the Sun are quite a clue.

They might have looked already—long ago, perhaps in the time of the dinosaurs or earlier— and given up.

A chemical map of Earth could show how we have moved some substances around and concentrated them in odd places.

Earth has lots of liquid water, which makes it a good place for life.

83

ACID RAIN FELL FOR 100 YEARS

As snowball Earth melted, ice turned to water and evaporated, leading to the worst weather ever.

Massive hurricanes tore across the land, waves 100 m (300 feet) tall smashed into the coast, and a torrential rainstorm lasted at least 100 years.

Water from the ice mixed with carbon dioxide from the volcanoes to make acid rain. It was so powerful it dissolved the rocks it fell onto, changing the geology of Earth.

Darling, we're not moving to Earth—the weather is dreadful!

WE BREATHE EARTH'S THIRD ATTEMPT AT AN ATMOSPHERE

Earth had a different atmosphere long ago—but lost it. The first atmosphere was mostly hydrogen-based gases, like the gas giants are now.

Lots of volcanoes erupting in the Earth's youth poured different gases into the atmosphere, so that it became mostly nitrogen, carbon dioxide, and water. That was the second atmosphere.

Finally, tiny bacteria producing oxygen changed the atmosphere again. They took in a lot of the carbon dioxide and pushed out oxygen. Green plants still do that. Now our atmosphere is about a fifth oxygen, which is lucky, as we need the oxygen to live.

OXYGEN WAS ONCE A POISON

All plants and animals living on Earth now need oxygen to breathe—but long ago oxygen killed off most of the things then living.

About 3.5 billion years ago, tiny microbes first started to photosynthesize, making oxygen from carbon dioxide and water using the energy of sunlight.

Now all plants do that, but at the time it was new. They filled the atmosphere with oxygen. No other microbes were used to oxygen and it poisoned them. Most died.

The microbes that make oxygen became the ancestors of the first plants. As other life developed, it used the oxygen—and here we are!

EARTH IS A GIANT MAGNET

The Earth's magnetic field is produced by liquid iron moving around solid iron at the Earth's core (see page 60). This turns the Earth into a magnet, with one magnetic pole near the Geographic North Pole and the other one near the Geographic South Pole.

The magnetic field extends out into space and affects the solar wind (particles streaming from the Sun).

Every now and then, the Earth's poles switch around, so the north magnetic pole ends up near the South Pole.

The last switch was 780,000 years ago, and many scientists think the Earth is gearing up for another switch. But it takes a long time to happen—more like 1,000 years than overnight!

EARTH'S GREAT AT RECYCLING

Many important chemicals on Earth are used again and again in different ways, and go back to where they started to be used again.

One example is the water cycle. Water evaporates from the sea, and forms clouds, which fall as rain over land. Some of the water is used by plants and animals and eventually released again, and the rest flows over the land into rivers that carry it back to the sea.

The water you drink today was once drunk by a dinosaur!

IN 1908, THE SKY EXPLODED

A massive explosion in the air over Russia called the Tunguska event was probably caused by a huge asteroid.

It flattened 2,000 square km (770 square miles) of forest—about 80 million trees—on June 30, 1908. Luckily, no one lived underneath.

It made a fireball 50–100 m (165–330 ft) across. Scientists think it was caused by an asteroid exploding as it passed through Earth's atmosphere at 15–30 km (9–19 miles) per second.

Asteroids this size might hit Earth every 100–200 years.

HOW TO MAKE A PLANET IN 4.5 BILLION YEARS

1 Like all the other planets, Earth started off as dust and gas whirling around the Sun. The dust and gas clumped into lumps.

2 The heaviest material stayed closest to the Sun, making the rocky planets—including Earth.

3 As the Earth-lump spun around and around, it became spherical. The heaviest bits went to the middle, making the iron core.

4 All the rocky planets started in the same way—but they've all turned out a bit different.

5 For 500 million years, Earth was struck by large asteroids and other space lumps.

6 Impact from space rocks and volcanic eruptions kept Earth's surface so hot the rock was molten and runny.

7 The scalding hot Earth started to cool and the outside formed a solid crust. Water pooled on the crust, making oceans.

8 Earth's iron core is slowly solidifying. The solid part grows 2.5 cm (1 in) every 25 years— but the molten part is still 2,300 km (1,430 miles) thick.

9 Over the last 100 million years, Earth's layer of molten rock (mantle) has cooled 20 °C (36 °F). It's cooling twice as fast as it used to.

10 Earth will be habitable for another 2–3 billion years. Then it's likely to drift too close to the Sun and get too hot for life.

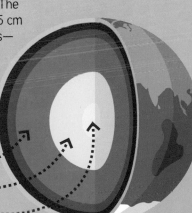

Mantle ·······
Liquid core ·······
Solid core ·······

EARTH'S NEAREST PLANET IS MARS—USUALLY.

Sometimes it's Venus. They swap around.

Mars, Venus, and Earth all orbit around the Sun at different speeds. That means sometimes Mars and Earth are on opposite sides of the Sun, 400 million km (248 million miles) apart.

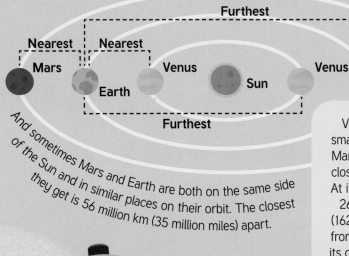

Furthest

Nearest | **Nearest**

Mars

Venus | **Venus** | **Mars**

Earth | **Sun**

Furthest

And sometimes Mars and Earth are both on the same side of the Sun and in similar places on their orbit. The closest they get is 56 million km (35 million miles) apart.

Venus is on a smaller orbit than Mars because it's closer to the Sun. At its furthest, it's 261 million km (162 million miles) from Earth, but at its closest it's only 40 million km (25 million miles) away.

THE INSIDE OF EARTH
SOMETIMES COMES OUT

When a volcano erupts, scorching hot, molten rock from inside the Earth pours out through a gap in the surface. While it's inside, it's called magma, but once it's outside, it's called lava.

Along with the lava, superheated water and gases come out of volcanoes. Volcanoes have helped make the landscape and the atmosphere by bringing material from deep inside the planet up to the surface.

Magma

Other planets and moons in the solar system also have volcanoes that let some of their insides out. Some spew up hot rock, and some spew out water or ice.

EARTH'S SEABED IS SLOWLY RECYCLED

The oceans have small rifts (cracks) running down the middle of the seabed, through which new rock oozes all the time. Old rock is pushed out of the way by the new rock, so the whole seabed slowly moves toward the shore.

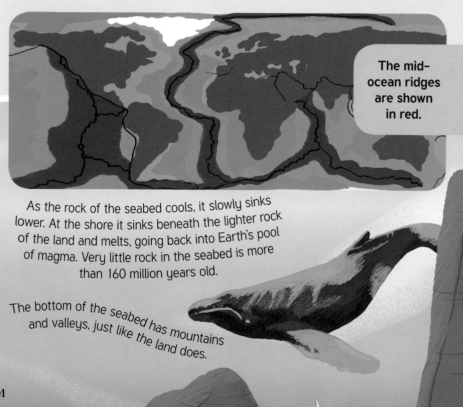

The mid-ocean ridges are shown in red.

As the rock of the seabed cools, it slowly sinks lower. At the shore it sinks beneath the lighter rock of the land and melts, going back into Earth's pool of magma. Very little rock in the seabed is more than 160 million years old.

The bottom of the seabed has mountains and valleys, just like the land does.

AMERICA AND EUROPE ARE DRIFTING APART

The Atlantic Ocean is growing wider at the rate of about 2.5 cm (1 in) a year as new seabed wells up from the middle of the Atlantic Ocean.

One rift in Earth's surface divides Europe and North America. It runs right through the middle of the island of Iceland, so Iceland will slowly be split in half.

On the other side of the world, the Pacific Ocean is getting narrower. One day in the distant future, America and Asia will be pushed together and the Pacific Ocean will close up—but not for hundreds of millions of years.

INDIA WAS ONCE AN ISLAND

The land on Earth moves all the time, but very slowly, as the tectonic plates are carried around by currents in the magma beneath.

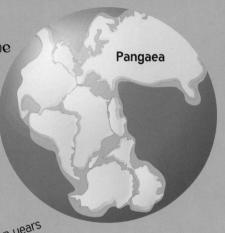

Pangaea

Over millions of years, the land all bunches up into a single giant continent and then breaks up and drifts apart again.

Last time it was all together was 200 million years ago, in a supercontinent called Pangaea.

India was once an island that has slowly drifted north. Its collision with Asia pushed up the Himalayas to make Earth's tallest mountain range.

Other mountain ranges were also made by parts of the Earth's crust crunching together and piling up.

YOU DON'T JUST HAVE TO WORRY ABOUT RAIN—space weather affects Earth, too

The "weather" in space is produced by bursts of energy of different kinds and particles from the Sun.

Space weather can affect GPS and communications satellites so that they don't work properly.

It can disrupt the electric power grid that brings electricity to your home and school. It can produce drag that makes satellites drift off their orbits slightly, too.

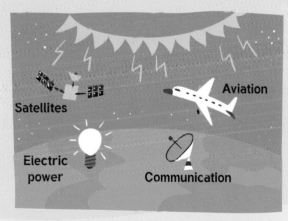

Satellites

Aviation

Electric power

Communication

And Earth's weather is affected by space weather. All of Earth's weather system depends on the Sun, so when the Sun does something odd, we can expect something odd down here.

MARS IS GETTING CLOSER!

In 2003, Mars came within 55.76 million km (34.65 million miles) of Earth—the closest it's been in 60,000 years.

It will get even closer in 2287 and even closer still in 2729 at 55.65 million km (34.58 million miles).

And some time around the year 25,000 it will be around 54.2 million km (33.68 million miles) away from Earth.

But Mars isn't on a slow collision course. The planets do a complicated dance around the Sun, with their orbits changing very slightly over patterns of thousands and even millions of years.

After 25,000 years, Mars will start to move a bit further away again.

EARTH'S ATMOSPHERE STRETCHES
10,000 KM INTO SPACE

But it's very thin at the top.

**Exosphere
ends at 10,000 km
(6,200 miles)**

**Thermosphere
ends at 600 km
(300 miles)**

**Mesosphere
ends at 85 km
(53 miles)**

**Stratosphere
ends at 50 km
(31 miles)**

**Troposphere—
ends at 8-18 km
(5-11 miles)**

The exosphere, the outer layer, is more than 9,330 km (5,800 miles) thick. The gases are so thin there they don't work like an atmosphere but are still held by Earth's gravity. The Moon and Mercury have an exosphere but no proper atmosphere below it.

The bit we live in is called the troposphere. It's 8 km (5 miles) thick at the poles and about 18 km (11 miles) thick at the equator. Most of the gases and nearly all the atmosphere's water—including clouds and rain—are in this bottom bit where we are.

THE EARTH IS COLDEST AT THE EDGES

The middle of the Earth is scorching, the magma is pretty hot, but the crust is a comfortable temperature to live on. The temperature drops quickly moving up through the atmosphere.

The temperature outside a plane in the middle of a flight is around −51 °C (−60 °F). That's just 11,000 m (35,000 ft) above the ground.

The average temperature on the ground is 14 °C (57 °F), but there's quite a range.

The hottest temperature ever recorded is 70.7°C (159°F) in Iran and the coldest is −89.2°C (−129°F) in Antarctica.

FISH FOSSILS ARE FOUND UP MOUNTAINS

As the plates of the Earth's crust move around, some crash into each other and the edges are pushed together and upward, making mountains.

The edges were previously coastline, so the rock at the tops of the highest mountains was once under the sea. Any fish fossilized in the coastal rock can end up on top of a mountain.

The rocks inland are much older than the rock beneath the sea, so this is where we find the oldest fossils. The oldest rocks are 4 billion years old—nearly as old as the Earth—although no fossils are quite that old.

EARTH IS
THE ONLY PLANET
WE KNOW TO HAVE LIFE

Tyrannosaurus rex

Dodo

None of the other planets or moons in the solar system is likely to have life, except just possibly tiny microbes.

There's been even more life in the past; over 99 percent of all species that have ever lived have died out.

It took just 250–500 million years before chemicals got together and made the earliest life forms …

… but another 3.5 billion years before large life forms started to grow.

Earth has lots of life—about 8.7 million different species.

Life probably started in the water, either deep in the sea or in pools.

There was no soil on Earth until living things moved onto the land. Soil is made from broken-down plant and animal matter.

That life started soon after the formation of Earth suggests it gets going easily on a planet with the right conditions.

Everything lived in the water until nearly 500 million years ago.

Humans like us appeared only 200,000 years ago.

103

The Moon was created
BY A MASSIVE
PLANETARY CRASH

Our Moon formed when a small planet or huge asteroid (space rock) crashed into Earth 4.5 billion years ago—only about 100 million years after Earth formed.

The Earth and Moon are made of exactly the same materials, so either the Moon is a chunk of the Earth, or they both formed from the same stuff.

One idea is that a small planet smashed into Earth, knocking out a huge chunk that became the Moon. The planet has been called Theia.

Or perhaps both Earth and the rogue planet vaporized (turned to gas), and Earth and the Moon both formed from the cooling mixture.

OUR MOON IS
BIG AND BEEFY

It's the largest moon belonging to a rocky planet. Mercury and Venus have no moons, and Mars's two moons are tiny by comparison with Earth's Moon.

There are only four larger moons in the whole solar system. Three belong to Jupiter and one to Saturn.

Moon	Planet	Mean diameter
Ganymede	Jupiter	5,268 km (3,273 miles)
Titan	Saturn	5,150 km (3,200 miles)
Callisto	Jupiter	4,821 km (3,002 miles)
Io	Jupiter	3,643 km (2,264 miles)
Moon	Earth	3,476 km (2,159 miles)

Only the dwarf planet Pluto has a larger moon for its size, at nearly 12% of its mass.

MASS OF MOONS
The gas and ice giants have loads of moons, but they never add up to more than one tenth of a percent (0.1%) of the mass of their planet. Our Moon, on its own, is 1 percent of the mass of Earth.

THE MOON'S

SURFACE IS PITTED WITH CRATERS FROM COLLISIONS WITH SPACE ROCKS.

The name "crater" was first used by Italian scientist Galileo in 1609. He took it from the Greek word for a cup for mixing water and wine.

Craters are named. Names included Robert, Gaston, and Isabel.

The Moon has been bombarded by rocks from space (meteors and asteroids) for billions of years, and it's still happening.

Most craters on the Moon were formed 3-4 billion years ago

Craters have a dip in the middle and a wall around the edge.

As there is no wind and rain to weather the craters, they remain as they are for billions of years.

In 2013, a rock weighing 40 kg (88 lb) hurtled into the Moon at 90,000 km/h (56,000 mph). It made a crater about 20 m (65 ft) across and the flash of the impact was visible from Earth without a telescope.

When a space rock crashes into the Moon, rock is blasted out of the surface, some of it melting in the intense heat of the impact.

The smallest craters are microscopic— too small to see with the naked eye. They have been seen in Moon rocks returned to Earth.

People once thought the Moon perfectly smooth; they didn't believe there could be anything imperfect in the heavens.

The area outside the craters is scattered with smashed rock and beads of glass, made when molten rock cools.

THE MOON HAS UPS AND DOWNS

The Moon has highlands and lowlands. Together, they make the patterns of dark and light we see when we look at the Moon.

The highlands are the light areas on the surface, and the low-lying areas are darker, made of rock rich in iron.

The highland rock is much older than the darker, lowland rock.

LAND AND SEA?

The low areas are flat plains called "maria" (seas). The highlands are called "terrae" (lands). The astronomer Johannes Kepler named them in the 1600s, thinking they were really areas of land and sea.

The Moon landing sites
ARE BEING PRESERVED

The sites of the Moon landings are "lunar heritage sites," similar to the "world heritage sites" that are protected special places on Earth.

The Sea of Tranquility area, with its abandoned Moon junk, will be left as an eternal memorial to our earliest explorations of the Moon.

When new probes are sent to crash into the Moon, they are aimed well away from the early landing sites to avoid damaging them.

HUMAN FOOTPRINTS ON THE MOON WILL STILL BE THERE I MILLIONS OF YEARS.

The Moon has very little atmosphere and no weather, such as rain and wind, to wipe out the tracks.

Its surface isn't recycled like the surface of Earth. Nothing changes...

People have left their marks on the Moon—in the form of footprints and vehicle tracks in the dust.

An asteroid or meteor crashing into just the right spot could destroy or cover the footprints—but otherwise they could last millions of years, or even as long as the Moon itself.

The Moon is
EXTREMELY DUSTY

It's entirely covered by a layer of small stones and dust called "regolith."

Regolith is rock that has been ground to dust or small stones by repeated collisions from asteroids and meteors. It's mixed with tiny blobs of glassy minerals formed when molten rocks cooled quickly.

It's because the Moon has a loose, dusty layer that the Apollo missions left footprints and tracks on the Moon. If it was solid rock, there would be none.

In some of the lowlands the regolith is just 2 m (6–7 ft) thick, but on the highlands it can be as deep as 20 m (66 ft).

THE FIRST SPACECRAFT ON THE MOON CRASH-LANDED

ON PURPOSE! The Soviet craft Luna 2 was deliberately crashed into the Moon's surface on September 13, 1959. It was the first object from Earth ever to land on another celestial body.

An earlier Luna 1 mission missed the Moon, sailing straight past, and is still moving around the Sun.

Luna 2 let out a cloud of gas as it neared the Moon that grew to 650 km (400 miles) wide. This let scientists on Earth track its progress by telescope.

Luna 2 carried two titanium balls made up of 5-sided shields called "pennants." An explosive charge in the middle was supposed to blow them apart, scattering the shields over the Moon's surface—but they probably vaporized on impact.

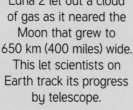

We always see the SAME SIDE OF THE MOON

No one saw the far side of the Moon until 1959, when the Soviet spacecraft Luna 3 flew around the back and sent photos of it.

The Moon takes as long to turn once on its axis as it does to travel all the way around the Earth, so the same side of the Moon is always visible from Earth.

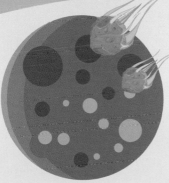

The other, hidden, side of the Moon has a much thicker and older crust and many more craters than "our" side. Meteors and asteroids have smashed through the thinner crust on our side, and hot liquid rock has flowed out and renewed the surface. On the other side, the crust is too thick to be punched through by space rocks.

The maria are just on
THE SIDE WE CAN SEE

On the near side, maria (flat plains) cover nearly a third of the surface, but on the far side, it's only a few percent.

HOT ROCKS!
The maria were never seas of water, but were once flooded with hot, molten rock (lava) which poured from volcanoes. It cooled and hardened to a flat surface. Some maria have been made by asteroids punching holes in the Moon's surface, allowing the lava inside to leak out.

MOON TREES
HAVE GROWN FROM
SPACEFARING SEEDS

Apollo 14 carried 500 tree seeds in on a trip around the Moon (but they didn't land). The seeds were from Loblolly Pine, Sycamore, Sweetgum, Redwood, and Douglas Fir trees.

Second-generation Moon trees, grown from seeds or cuttings from the original Moon trees, are growing in the USA, England, Italy, and Switzerland.

Returned to Earth, nearly all the seeds germinated and have grown into trees. Most Moon trees are growing in the USA, but there are also Moon trees in Japan, Brazil, and Switzerland.

115

ASTRONAUTS BROUGHT LUMPS OF THE MOON HOME WITH THEM

Six Apollo Moon missions brought back 2,196 samples of moon rock and dust, weighing 382 kg (841.5 lb). The largest chunk weighs a hefty 11.7 kg (25.8 lb)—but on the Moon, with lower gravity, it weighed only 1.95 kg (4.3 lb).

NASA's samples of Moon rock are kept at the Johnson Space Center in Houston, Texas, and sent out to scientists when they need them for research. About 400 samples are sent out every year.

THE MOON
squashed its sister—maybe
In 2011, some scientists suggested that Earth once had two moons.

The second, smaller, moon would have been 1,270 km (790 miles) across—about one third the size of the surviving Moon.

It would have lasted about 70 million years before crashing into the present Moon at a speed of 2–3 km per second (1.2–1.9 miles per second).

Instead of making a crater, the unlucky moon would have been smeared all over one side of the survivor.

This could be why the far side of the Moon has a much thicker crust than the near side.

You can lose weight immediately
BY GOING TO THE MOON

Gravity on the Moon is only about one sixth of Earth's gravity. That means that an astronaut who weighs 82 kg (180 lb) on Earth will weigh only 14 kg (30 lb) on the Moon.

Lower gravity means astronauts can leap and bounce in ways they could never do on Earth. But they also fall over more—people need at least 15 percent of Earth's gravity to give their bodies a good idea of which way is "up," so the Moon has barely enough.

Everything else weighs less, too, so astronauts can pick up objects that would be far too heavy for them to lift on Earth.

THE "MAN IN THE MOON" could be a toad or a rabbit

People have always seen pictures in the patterns on the full Moon, but they haven't all seen the same thing.

Some have seen a person with a bundle of sticks, an old man with a lantern, or a woman with a fancy hairstyle and jewels.

And it's not always a person. In China, Japan, and Korea, people see a rabbit making something in a pot—maybe medicine or rice cakes. Other cultures have seen a buffalo, moose, frog, toad, or dragon.

THE MOON HAS MOONQUAKES

Apollo astronauts placed seismometers on the Moon. These are instruments to measure vibrations in the ground.

The readings they sent back to Earth showed 28 moonquakes of four different types between 1969 and 1977.

Most earthquakes last just a few seconds, and even the longest are over in two minutes. But moonquakes can keep on going for 10 minutes.

If we ever build a space station on the Moon, it will have to be made of slightly flexible material so that it isn't cracked by moonquakes.

ONLY TWELVE PEOPLE HAVE
ever set foot on the Moon.

Another twelve astronauts have flown to the Moon and around it but have not landed on it. That means only 24 people in total have ever seen the far side of the Moon.

There was always one astronaut who stayed in orbit around the Moon while others landed. The earliest missions didn't have a lander at all.

Six of the astronauts also drove rovers, or "moon buggies," over the surface. No one has landed on the Moon more than once.

All twelve people were male, white Americans.

MOON STATISTICS

The Moon travels around Earth at 1 km per second (0.64 miles per second)—or 3,600 km/h (2,304 mph).

Flying around the moon, an astronaut covers the same distance as a plane flying from New York to London.

The volume of the Moon is only 2 percent (one fiftieth) the volume of Earth.

Moon

Pluto

Earth

Our Moon is larger than the dwarf planet Pluto. Pluto is only two-thirds the size of the Moon at 2,370 km (1,473 miles) across.

The first person to calculate the size of the Moon was the Greek mathematician Aristarchus 2,200 years ago. He thought it was half as wide as the Earth, though it's actually a quarter as wide. Not bad, though!

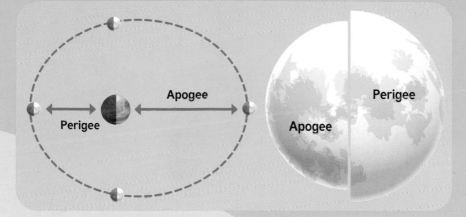

The Moon's orbit around Earth is not a perfect circle. At its closest (called "perigee"), the Moon is 363,300 km (225,740 miles) away. When it's furthest away (called "apogee"), it's 405,500 km (251,970 miles) from Earth.

When the Moon is closer to Earth, it looks bigger. The biggest full moon is 14 percent larger and 30 percent brighter than the smallest. The biggest full moons are called "supermoons."

The Moon's very thin atmosphere is made of helium, argon, possibly neon, ammonia, methane, and carbon dioxide. It's nothing like Earth's atmosphere, which has just 1% argon and tiny amounts of the others.

The Moon moves about 3.8 cm (1.2 in) further away from the Earth every year.

THE FIRST FLAG PLANTED ON THE MOON FELL OVER

The astronauts of the first Moon landing in 1969, Neil Armstrong and Buzz Aldrin, planted an American flag on the surface of the Moon.

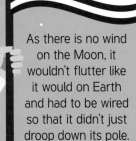

As there is no wind on the Moon, it wouldn't flutter like it would on Earth and had to be wired so that it didn't just droop down its pole.

But the blast from the departing spacecraft blew the flag down. The glorious memorial of humankind's first Moon landing was a bit of a damp squib in the end.

IT WOULD TAKE 17 DAYS to fly to the Moon by jumbo jet

Or it would if you could do that!

It's 384,000 km (240,000 miles) from Earth to the Moon, and a Boeing 747 travels at around 965 km/h (600 mph). If you could go by car at 80 km/h (50 mph), it would take 200 days—nearly seven months!

A rocket going to the Moon doesn't follow a straight path.

Instead, it goes part or all of the way around the Earth and the Moon.

The Apollo spacecraft each took only 3–4 days to reach the Moon.

125

THE MOON HAD HUGE
VOLCANIC ERUPTIONS

Volcanoes no longer pour out scorching, semi-liquid rock on the Moon, but they did once.

The huge, flat plains of the maria are vast lava floods that have cooled and turned solid.

The Moon's large volcanoes have probably been dead for about a billion years. But some much smaller ones seem to have erupted more recently—perhaps as little as 18 million years ago. And they might erupt again, one day.

The Moon and Sun look exactly the same size in the sky

The Moon is 3,474 km (2,159 miles) across, while the Sun is 1.4 million km (864,576 miles) across—so the Sun is 400 times wider than the Moon.

But the Moon is much closer than the Sun, so it looks big. While the Moon is only 384,400 km (238,900 miles) from Earth, the Sun is 390 times as far away. Eclipsed!

Because they look the same size, the Moon can completely cover the Sun in a solar eclipse, making it dark on Earth.

A GOLF BALL GOES A LONG, LONG WAY ON THE MOON

Apollo 14 astronaut Alan Shepard smuggled a makeshift golf club and two golf balls to the Moon in 1971, hoping to make a record-breaking stroke.

His first shot was disappointing, but the second flew more than 183 m (200 yd), helped by low gravity and no air.

He fixed the head of a golf club to a piece of NASA equipment for collecting rocks. Then he covered the head with a sock so that he could get it onto the spacecraft without anyone noticing.

The golf balls are still on the Moon.

The Moon's gravity PULLS THE WATER OF EARTH'S OCEANS, making the tides

At high tide, the sea comes further up the beach and at low tide it doesn't come as far up. The reason is that the Moon is pulling the water!

As the Earth turns, the water on the side closest to the Moon is pulled toward the Moon. The water on the opposite side also "piles up."

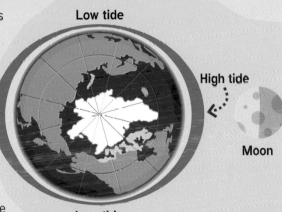

Low tide

High tide

Moon

Low tide

Each bit of coast has two high tides each day, once when that area is closest to the Moon and once when it's furthest away.

129

We measure the distance TO THE MOON BY BOUNCING a laser beam off its surface

Reflector

There are five special collections of glass prisms called "retroreflectors" on the Moon's surface. They were left there by the NASA Apollo missions and the Soviet Luna missions.

Retroflector sites

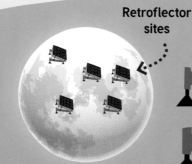

Retroflector

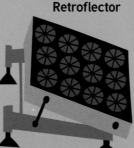

Scientists on Earth direct a laser beam to a retroreflector and time how long it takes to be reflected back to Earth. From this they can work out exactly how far away the retroreflector is—and so how far it is to the Moon.

THE MOON DOESN'T REALLY "SHINE"

The Moon is only illuminated when sunlight falls on it; it doesn't "shine" out light of its own. The part that has no sunlight falling on it is dark.

At full moon, the Sun shines straight onto the Moon and we can see all of it.

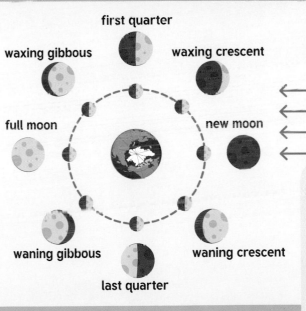

first quarter

waxing gibbous

waxing crescent

full moon

new moon

sunlight

waning gibbous

waning crescent

last quarter

As the Moon goes around the Earth, it seems to change shape. It goes from a thin crescent to a full circle and back in eight "phases." When the Sun is hidden behind the Moon, the Moon is all in shadow and barely visible; this is a new moon.

The part of the Moon that has no sunlight falling on it is dark, and we can only see the parts lit by the Sun.

THE LAST VISITOR LEFT THE MOON
DECEMBER 14, 1972

NASA's Apollo 17 was the last crewed mission to the Moon.

Eugene Cernan was the last person to leave the Moon, on December 14, 1972.

All the astronauts who have landed on the Moon went between the first Moon landing in 1969 and the last in 1972—a period of just over three years.

Rabbit on the Moon

The Chinese Chang Zheng 3B mission carried a robotic rover to the Moon called Yutu (Jade Rabbit) in December 2013. It was the longest working rover on the Moon, surviving for 31 months.

THE MOON'S DAYTIME IS TWO WEEKS LONG

A day is the time it takes a celestial body to turn on its own axis. Earth's day is 24 hours long. The Moon takes 27.3 days to turn once on its axis, so a Moon-day is 27.3 Earth-days long.

Each half of the Moon faces the Sun for half that time (two weeks). The Moon has extreme temperatures, as it has a long time to heat up in the day and to cool down at night.

Earth goes around the Sun once in 365 days, which is a year. The Moon's "year" is the 29 days it takes to go around the Earth, which is barely longer than its day.

133

The first food and drink consumed on the Moon were "holy"

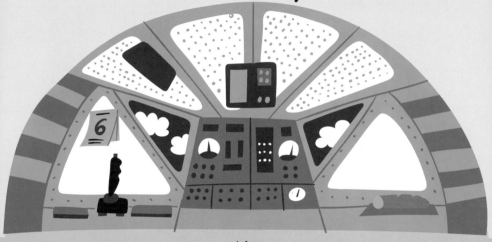

Apollo 11 astronaut Buzz Aldrin smuggled holy communion wine and a communion wafer onto the spacecraft and took communion on the Moon.

Aldrin asked over the radio for a few moments of silence and for people to "contemplate the events of the past few hours, and to give thanks." He did not tell NASA about his communion until after the mission.

The communion wine curled up the side of the cup because of the low gravity.

THERE IS WATER ON THE MOON

Everyone knows the Moon is bone dry— but only on the surface.

Scientists examining tiny glass beads made of volcanic rock on the Moon found small amounts of water locked into them. The volcanic rock is widespread on the Moon.

Water trapped in rock on the Moon is not easy to spot, but it might go down to great depths. The Moon might contain enough locked-away water to make an ocean 90 cm (3 ft) deep over the whole surface.

There's even ice in at least one deep crater at the Moon's South Pole. Sunlight never reaches the bottom and water ice can lurk there without thawing for billions of years.

There's a **DEAD** astronomer on the Moon—**OR PART OF ONE**

The American astronomer Eugene Shoemaker always wanted to be an astronaut, but a medical problem made it impossible. After he died, his ashes were packed onto the Lunar Prospector lander, which was crashed into the south pole of the Moon on July 31, 1999. He is still the only person "buried" on the Moon.

EUGENE SHOEMAKER

BORN APRIL 28, 1928

DIED JULY 18, 1997

Not all of Shoemaker was sent to the Moon—just 28 g (1 oz) of his ashes made the trip, packed into a special capsule wrapped in brass foil, etched with his name and dates.

THE MOON HAS A TINY BIT OF ATMOSPHERE

Atmosphere is a layer of gas around a planet (or moon). Our Moon has a very, very thin atmosphere.

If you collected a jug of Earth-atmosphere and a jug of thin Moon-atmosphere, the Earth-jug would contain 10,000 billion times as many molecules (particles) as the Moon-jug.

Earth

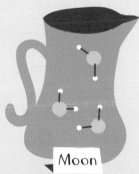

Moon

We wouldn't be able to breathe on the Moon, even if the atmosphere was much thicker, as it doesn't have the same gases as Earth's atmosphere.

The Incas thought a **JAGUAR** ate the Moon

When the Earth is lined up between the Sun and the Moon, the Earth's shadow falls across the full moon, turning it red in a lunar eclipse.

The Incas of South America used to believe it was a sign that a jaguar was eating the Moon. They thought that after eating the Moon, the jaguar might eat all the animals on Earth, so they carried spears to threaten the jaguar and shouted at the eclipse.

The Ancient Egyptians thought a female pig swallowed the Moon, and in Ancient China a three-legged toad was blamed.

THE SKY IS BLACK
in daytime on the Moon

On Earth, the sky is black at night and blue in the daytime.

The blue is produced by the Earth's atmosphere scattering light. The Moon has far too little atmosphere to scatter sunlight. So standing on the Moon and looking into space, you would see just space, in all its blackness.

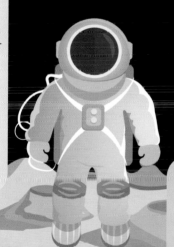

Most photos taken from the Moon don't show stars because the astronauts landed in daytime. As each day lasts two weeks on the Moon, it was never night. The Sun was too bright for stars to show up.

The night sky seen from the Moon is always full of stars—far more stars than you could ever see from Earth. With no light pollution or atmosphere, the stars are crystal-clear.

139

THE MOON COMES OUT IN THE DAYTIME

The Moon is above the horizon for roughly 12 hours a day, rising and setting once a day.

The Moon is obviously in the sky all the time, but people wrongly assume that we see it only at night. It's often visible in the daytime, too.

It often either rises before sunset or sets after sunrise, so it overlaps with daylight and is not always out all night.

At full moon, the Moon is directly opposite the Sun, so then it really is only visible at night.

There is a work of art on the Moon

It's a statuette known as the Fallen Astronaut, made by the Belgian sculptor Paul Van Hoeydonck.

The stylized human figure, 8.5 cm (3.3 in) tall, is made of light metal.

It commemorates the 14 American and Soviet astronauts known to have died. There is also a plaque listing their names.

BASSETT, CHARLES A. II
BELYAYEV, PAVEL I.
CHAFFEE, ROGER B.
DOBROVOLSKY, GEORGI T.
FREEMAN, THEODORE C.
GAGARIN, YURI A.
GIVENS, EDWARD G., Jr.
GRISSOM, VIRGIL I.
KOMOROV, VLADIMIR M.
PATSAYEV, VIKTOR I.
SEE, ELLIOT M Jr.
VOLKOV, VLADISLAV N
WHITE, EDWARDS H. II
WILLIAMS, CLIFTON C. Jr.

David Scott of Apollo 15 smuggled the statuette to the Moon and placed it secretly, not telling NASA until afterward.

Later, NASA asked the sculptor to make another copy, which is displayed in the National Air and Space Museum.

WE CAN FIND CHUNKS
of the Moon on Earth

Meteorites are rocks from space that fall to Earth.

Many meteorites that land on Earth are from the Moon—so they're bits of moon rock that have made their way here.

Moon meteorites—or lunaites—are chunks of rock smashed out of the moon by asteroids crashing into the surface and spraying bits out into space.

"Shooting stars" are meteors burning up as they streak through Earth's atmosphere

THERE COULD BE FOSSILS ON THE MOON

But not fossils of Moon-creatures, fossils from Earth.

Although there is no life on the Moon, it might hide fossils of early life on Earth. Earth meteors are chunks of rock knocked out of the Earth by asteroid impacts and hurled into space. They might have carried microscopic fossils to the Moon.

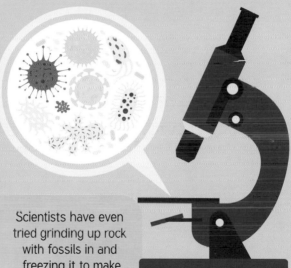

Scientists have even tried grinding up rock with fossils in and freezing it to make fake meteorites to see if rocks smashing into the Moon could deliver fossils intact.

If we ever find any fossils on the Moon, we shouldn't get too excited, as they might have come from Earth.

143

WE MIGHT BUILD A BASE ON THE MOON

It could be used as a jumping-off point for other space trips or a research station. But it would need to be a very special place.

The temperature on the Moon is not nice. It can get as hot as 127°C (260°F) in the daytime and drop to −173°C (−279°F) in the night. A moonbase would need to be well insulated and heated or cooled.

People need air to breathe, so any Moon base would have to be completely sealed to keep the air in, and able to recycle air.

There is no liquid water, but colonists might be able to extract water that is locked inside rocks or frozen into ices.

144

THE MOON IS BLUE—
"once in a blue moon"

In the phrase "once in a blue moon" a blue moon means means "rarely."
A blue moon is the second full moon in one calendar month. As there are 29 days between full moons, it's just possible for a month to have two.

But sometimes the Moon really does look blue. Dust or smoke in the atmosphere can disrupt the light coming from the Moon, making it blue.

The Moon also looks red during a lunar eclipse (see page 138).

THE MOON IS SHRINKING

Cracks and ridges in the Moon's surface suggest that it's been shrinking in the last billion years.

When the Moon first formed, it was scalding hot—indeed, molten. As it cooled, it shrank (because hot material takes up more space than the same material when it's cold).

The Moon has probably shrunk by about 183 m (600 ft) across its width.

The Moon has one of the largest impact craters IN THE SOLAR SYSTEM

The Aitken basin, near the Moon's south pole, is 2,500 km (1,600 miles) across.

From the lowest point of the basin's floor to the highest point of the surrounding wall, is more than 15 km (9.3 miles). That's twice as high as Mount Everest, the tallest mountain on Earth.

It was made by an asteroid perhaps 170 km (105 miles) across smashing into the Moon about 3.9 billion years ago. It gouged a hole 8 km (5 miles) deep in the Moon's surface, and pushed up walls of rock around the hole.

NO ONE CAN OWN PART OF THE MOON

Some companies claim to sell areas of land on the Moon, and take people's money for it, but they have no rights to any of the Moon and the "ownership" is not recognized.

FOR SALE

In 1967 the international Outer Space Treaty declared that no one can own any part of outer space, including the Moon.

One man from Germany claims the Moon was given to his family in 1756 by the King of Prussia, Frederick the Great.

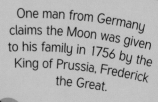

ASTRONAUTS ON THE MOON DID
AN EXPERIMENT SUGGESTED 400 YEARS AGO

Galileo dropped two spheres of different masses at the same time from a tower to show that heavy and light objects fall at the same speed. He thought this would also work with a cannonball and feather if there was no air to slow the feather down.

Apollo 15 astronaut David Scott dropped a feather and a hammer on the Moon in 1971. There is no air in space, and they did both hit the ground at the same time.

The feather was from a falcon called Baggins, who was an Air Force Academy mascot.

THERE'S A LOT OF STUFF ON THE MOON

Astronauts bring very little back, however, as they need their craft to be as light as possible for take off.

For 4.5 billion years, the Moon was a garabage-free zone—then people started going there. Now there's around 180,000 kg (400,000 lb) of clutter there.

A commemorative plaque attached to a leg of the abandoned Apollo 11 lander bears the words:

Even expensive cameras were not worth bringing home. A photographer looking for a great vintage camera from the 1970s could find some good stuff on the Moon.

"HERE MEN FROM THE PLANET EARTH FIRST SET FOOT UPON THE MOON JULY 1969 A.D."
WE CAME IN PEACE FOR ALL MANKIND.

We've left more than 70 vehicles on the Moon, including crashed spacecraft, used rovers, and discarded modules of craft.

Tools including hammers, rakes, and shovels were all left behind by the astronauts.

Apollo 11 astronauts left a satchel holding medals commemorating two Soviet cosmonauts, who died in 1967 and 1968, Vladimir Komarov and Yuri Gagarin.

The hammer and feather from the Galileo demonstration, and Alan Shepard's golf balls (see page 128) are still there.

A gold pin in the shape of an olive branch (an international symbol of peace) was left as a reminder that the Apollo missions were peaceful.

Another commemorative object is a patch from the Apollo 1 mission, which had burst into flames before its launch, killing three astronauts.

Some of the stuff left behind is really not very nice—used wet wipes, empty space-food packages, and 96 bags of human waste and vomit. Yuk!

LIFE ON THE MOON?

The idea that there could be life on the Moon is very old.

Astronomers in the early days of the telescope wondered whether the light patches on the Moon might be land and the dark patches ocean, either of which could perhaps hold living creatures.

The Moon has hardly any atmosphere and no liquid water on the surface—but those are recent discoveries.

The astronomer Johannes Kepler, in a letter in 1610, suggested that the creatures that live on the Moon have large bodies and make large, circular buildings that can be seen through a telescope.

Some of the ancient Greeks suggested nearly 2,500 years ago that the Moon was home to animals and plants like those on Earth but "larger and more beautiful."

Some people even today think NASA is hiding evidence that aliens have visited the Moon and even built a base there. There is absolutely no evidence that this is true.

In 1856, astronomer Peter Hansen suggested there could be life on the far side of the Moon, out of sight of Earth. The theory was popular for only about 12 years.

Nothing we recognize could live on the Moon. But it might be possible to build a base on the Moon for humans to live in, with its own atmosphere and a supply of food and water. We could be the life on the Moon!

THE FIRST PLANET DISCOVERED SINCE THE STONE AGE WAS URANUS

A German-English amateur astronomer called William Herschel spotted Uranus in 1781.

He wanted to name it after the king of England, so Uranus could have been called George.

George was pleased, and gave Herschel a lot of money. He used it to build bigger and better telescopes and became a full-time astronomer who made other important discoveries, but he never found another planet.

THE WHOLE SOLAR
SYSTEM FORMED FROM A
cloud of dust and gas

The Sun and all the planets and moons of the solar system formed 4.5 billion years ago from a huge, whirling cloud of dust and gas.

Bits of matter in the disk started to clump together. The heavier the lumps got, the more matter they attracted. The biggest lumps eventually became the eight planets and their moons.

THE INNER PLANETS ARE PRETTY DENSE

The solar system has four rocky planets and four made mostly of gas or ice.

The rocky planets—Mercury, Venus, Earth, and Mars—are nearest the Sun. The gassy planets are far, far bigger and much further away.

Mercury

Earth

Venus

Mars

Uranus

Saturn

Neptune

Jupiter

What the planets are made of relates to how they formed from the whirling cloud of gas and dust. Close to the Sun, it was too hot for the gases of the gassy planets to condense (squeeze together) and form into lumps. These light gases were carried further out and could condense only in a much colder region. Rock can be solid at much higher temperatures, though.

THE PLANET URANUS LIES ON ITS SIDE

It's the only planet that does so. It might have been knocked sideways by a collision with something billions of years ago.

It's "north" and "south" poles are in the east and west, as its axis (the line about which it rotates) is tilted at nearly 98 degrees.

Uranus takes 84 Earth-years to orbit the Sun. First one pole and then the other points toward the Sun for 42 years (half a Uranus-year). Just a narrow band near the equator gets a normal day/night sequence for part of the year.

Uranus has faint rings, which go from top to bottom.

THREE MEN IN YEMEN CLAIM TO OWN MARS

In 1997, three men from Yemen sued NASA for "invading" Mars by landing on it.

They say that their families inherited Mars from ancestors who lived 3,000 years ago. They based their claim on myths from early civilizations that died out long ago in ancient Saudi Arabia.

NASA did not agree that the men own Mars, and plan to continue exploring the planet.

Russian boy Boriska Kipriyanovich says he was once a Martian and has been reborn on Earth. From early childhood, he has told his parents about life on Mars, where he says the Martians live underground.

PLANETS MAKE TINY ECLIPSES

The planets Mercury and Venus are closer to the Sun than Earth, so sometimes they pass directly between us and the Sun. This is called a transit.

A transit is just like an eclipse, but much smaller. The planets are too small to blot out the Sun as the Moon does (see page 127). Mercury or Venus shows as just a tiny black spot crawling across the face of the Sun.

The other planets are further from the Sun than Earth so never pass between the two.

image of Sun on paper

binoculars

keep cap on unused side

to Sun

It's dangerous to look at the Sun, but you can use binoculars to project an image onto a wall or sheet of paper and watch the transit as a little shadow crossing the Sun.

MERCURY IS BARELY BIGGER
THAN OUR MOON

The Moon is 70 percent the size of Mercury, which is just 4,878 km (3,030 miles) across. And it's shrinking! New cracks over the surface appear as the hot inside cools and shrinks.

Mercury is about 58 million km (36 million miles) from the Sun—just over a third as far away as Earth, and the closest planet.

As the time taken by Mercury to turn on its axis is 59 Earth-days long, the planet's night and day are around 29½ Earth-days.

Jupiter may have destroyed a dwarf planet

Its remains orbit the Sun between Mars and Jupiter as billions or even trillions of chunks of rock called the Asteroid Belt.

Some of the asteroids made from the shattered dwarf planets are big enough to qualify as dwarf planets themselves.

Mars

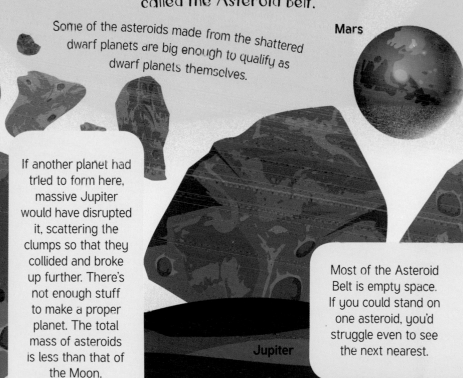

If another planet had tried to form here, massive Jupiter would have disrupted it, scattering the clumps so that they collided and broke up further. There's not enough stuff to make a proper planet. The total mass of asteroids is less than that of the Moon.

Jupiter

Most of the Asteroid Belt is empty space. If you could stand on one asteroid, you'd struggle even to see the next nearest.

VISITING OTHER WORLDS

Life would be very different on other worlds in our solar system.

If you could stand on Saturn—which you can't—you would see its rings as bands right across the sky.

On Pluto, you would weigh just one fifteenth of your weight on Earth.

You couldn't stand up on Jupiter as there's no solid surface. Instead, you would sink 60,000 km (37,000 miles) through gas and then thick soupy gloop before perhaps reaching a solid core.

On Venus, you would be crushed under atmospheric pressure 93 times that on Earth—and burned by the acidic clouds.

If you lived on Uranus, you would only get one birthday, at the most! As Uranus takes 84 Earth-years to orbit the Sun, only a single whole Uranus-year would pass in a human lifetime.

If you lived on Neptune, you might spend your entire life in its 80-year summer—but you could be unlucky and spend your whole life in winter.

162

If you lived on one of Jupiter's moons, such as Europa, Jupiter would loom massively in the sky, far larger than anything we see from Earth.

If you were on Mars, you could watch Earth's transit as it crossed in front of the Sun.

On Mercury, the Sun would look three times as big as it does on Earth.

On the dwarf planet Sedna, you'd only get a birthday once every 11,400 years.

Pluto is 4.8 billion km (3 billion miles) away, so it gets a lot less sunlight than Earth. But it's not completely dark—there's as much light at midday on Pluto as there is on Earth just after sunset.

You'd need a coat—or a cold drink—on Mercury. The temperature swings wildly between day and night. The side facing the Sun (day) gets scorching hot, at 427 °C (801 °F), and the side facing away (night) gets freezing cold—down to -173 °C (-279 °F).

If you visited Jupiter or Saturn, the sky would be full of moons! Jupiter has 79! They wouldn't all be visible at once, as some would be the other side of the planet—but can you imagine seeing even 30 moons in the sky?

MOONS CAN WORK AS SHEPHERDS

Just like a sheepdog herding a flock of sheep, moons control where the dust and rocks in a planet's rings go.

On an even bigger scale, planets keep their orbits around the Sun clear of chunks. It's part of their job as a planet—if they don't do it, they don't count as a planet.

PEOPLE ONCE THOUGHT ALIENS BUILT CANALS ON MARS

In 1877, Italian astronomer Giovanni Schiaparelli drew the first map of Mars. He was convinced he could see straight lines criss-crossing the surface of Mars. He called them canali, which means "channels," but people who didn't speak Italian thought that meant canals.

By 1909, astronomers with better telescopes showed there were no canals. But by then the idea of life on Mars had taken root. Science fiction writers wrote about aliens on Mars, and Martians came into existence—at least in books and movies!

PLANETS DON'T TWINKLE

One way that you can tell stars and planets apart without a telescope is by watching for twinkling. Stars twinkle, but planets don't.

Venus

Stars create their own light; planets just reflect the light of the Sun (our star).

How much light is reflected and gets back to us depends on how far away the planet is and what it's made of. Some surfaces reflect more light than others. A dark planet will reflect so little light it's hard to see. Mercury reflects only about one twentieth of the light that falls on it.

It's Venus's atmosphere that reflects light, while Mercury is dark rock.

Stars = twinkle

Planets ≠ twinkle

Mercury

THE PLANET NEPTUNE WAS ONLY DISCOVERED LAST YEAR

—if you think in Neptune-years.

Neptune was first seen in 1846, which is more than 170 Earth-years ago. But Neptune is so far from the Sun that it takes about 165 Earth-years to go round it once, so it's only just completed one circuit (one year) since it was first discovered. It's the outermost planet of the solar system—so far.

Neptune spins quite quickly on its axis, so its day is just 16 hours and 6 minutes long.

That means it has more than 87,000 days in its year. It's a long time between birthdays.

There are lots of moons

Earth isn't the only planet with a Moon.
However, it's the only planet that has just one moon.

Mercury and Venus don't have any moons, but the gas and ice giants have lots of moons.

Saturn and Jupiter both have lots, including moons that look like a potato, a meatball, and a sponge. Why have a boring old round moon if you don't have to?

Saturn's moon Hyperion looks like a sponge

A moon is a natural satellite—a body, usually made of rock, which orbits around something which is itself in orbit around the Sun (usually a planet).

Saturn's Prometheus looks like a potato!

If Jupiter were 80 times bigger, IT COULD BE A STAR

Jupiter, a gas giant, is made mostly of hydrogen, the same as the Sun. But to work as a star, it would need to be even bigger.

In a big ball of hydrogen, gravity pulls everything inward under enough pressure to crush the atoms together. That's a process called nuclear fusion, and it's how stars produce heat and light.

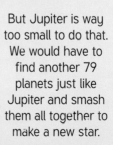

But Jupiter is way too small to do that. We would have to find another 79 planets just like Jupiter and smash them all together to make a new star.

MOONS: BIG, SMALL, AND TRULY WEIRD

The gas giants have loads of moons; Saturn has at least 61 and Jupiter at least 79. Because the planets are so large, their gravity reaches far into space, letting them capture passing lumps of rock and ice and dragging them into orbit as moons.

Jupiter's moon Io is the most volcanic place in the solar system. It has 400 active volcanoes, some of them shooting smelly fumes of sulfur 500 km (310 miles) out into space.

Some of the moons of the gas and ice giants are as big as small planets, but others are barely 1 km (0.6 mile) across.

Moon

Rhea **Dione**

Earth **Mercury** **Callisto**

Mars **Ganymede**

The largest moon in the solar system is Ganymede, which belongs to Jupiter. It has a thin atmosphere of oxygen and a salty ocean 200 km (124 miles) below the surface.

Even asteroids can have their own tiny moons.

The surface of Saturn's moon Enceladus is 99% water (or, rather, ice). It has ice volcanoes that shoot 250 kg (550 lb) of water into space every second.

Saturn's moon Atlas is fat—it has a thick girdle of rock around the middle, built up by bits sticking to it from one of Saturn's rings. It makes Atlas twice as wide as it is tall, at 40 x 20 km (25 x 12.5 miles).

One of the coldest places in the solar system is Triton, a moon of Neptune. The temperature drops to a bone-chilling −235 °C (−391 °F).

Not happy with just being super-chilly, Triton is a bit of an oddball because it rotates the opposite way to Neptune. Most moons rotate in the same direction as their planets.

Moons can be rocky or icy. Icy moons often have a liquid layer underneath. Most, maybe all, moons have a solid rocky or iron core right in the middle.

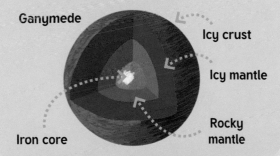

Ganymede

Icy crust

Icy mantle

Rocky mantle

Iron core

171

SOME OF SATURN'S RINGS ARE ONLY 10 M (33 FT) THICK

But they are 400,000 km (240,000 miles) across—further than the distance from Earth to the Moon. There are 500–1,000 separate rings, with some big and small gaps between them.

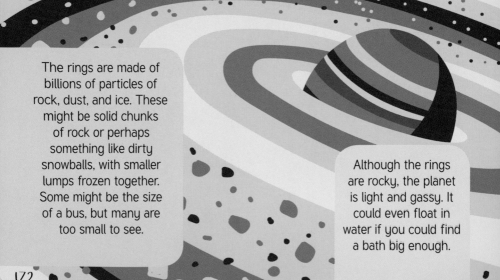

The rings are made of billions of particles of rock, dust, and ice. These might be solid chunks of rock or perhaps something like dirty snowballs, with smaller lumps frozen together. Some might be the size of a bus, but many are too small to see.

Although the rings are rocky, the planet is light and gassy. It could even float in water if you could find a bath big enough.

Mars is rusty

It's known as the red planet, and its surface has red rocks and soil because there's a lot of iron oxide—rust—in them.

Demos

Phobos

Mars has two moons, but they're tiny. Phobos is 22.2 km (13.8 miles) across and Demos is just 12.6 km (7.8 miles) across. Both look rather like potatoes—they aren't large enough to have spun themselves into spheres.

Mars is much smaller than Earth—it's 6,791 km (4,220 miles) across, or just over half the width of Earth. Mars would fit inside Earth six times.

173

VENUS'S DAY IS
LONGER THAN ITS YEAR

Venus, the second planet from the Sun, takes 224 days to orbit around it.

But it turns on its own axis so slowly that it takes 243 Earth-days to make one full rotation. It doesn't complete even one "day" before it's been right around the Sun.

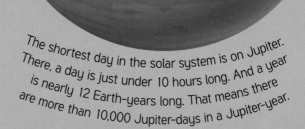

The shortest day in the solar system is on Jupiter. There, a day is just under 10 hours long. And a year is nearly 12 Earth-years long. That means there are more than 10,000 Jupiter-days in a Jupiter-year.

TWO PLANETS TURN THE WRONG WAY

Venus and Uranus both rotate from east to west (clockwise, seen looking down at the north pole), while all the other planets go the other way.

All planets orbit the Sun going west to east, so it seems they should all turn on their axes the same way. But Venus and Uranus have gone wrong.

They were probably both knocked over by an early collision with a large asteroid. Uranus is still on its side, but Venus might have been entirely turned over—so it's still spinning the same way, but now the top is at the bottom!

Mercury

Venus

Earth

Mars

Jupiter

Saturn

Uranus

Neptune

Some moons have
BEEN KIDNAPPED

Planets can get moons in one of three ways:

- the moon can form alongside the planet from the start

- the planet can "kidnap" a passing space rock, dragging it into orbit to be its moon

- the moon can be a chunk knocked out of the planet in a massive collision, as might have happened to Earth

There are probably moons acquired in all three ways in our solar system. After all, there are about 200 moons just around the planets and dwarf planets, so there's plenty of room for variety.

MOON BAG

MARS HAS A VOLCANO THE SIZE OF FRANCE

Olympus Mons, on Mars, is the largest volcano in the solar system.

It's more than 22 km (13.5 miles) tall, while the tallest mountain on Earth, Mount Everest, is just over a third that size at 8.8 km (5.5 miles) high. Olympus Mons is not only tall—it's 100 times the volume of the largest volcano on Earth.

Olympus Mons

As a shield volcano, Olympus Mons has shallow slopes that build up as lava slowly leaks out. That's why it can cover an area the size of France on a planet much smaller than Earth.

Olympus Mons has not erupted for around 25 million years, and appears to be dead.

Astronomers watched a comet smash into Jupiter

—AND DID NOTHING!

It didn't end nicely. The comet Shoemaker-Levy 9 had been captured by Jupiter's gravity 20–30 years earlier.

Jupiter kept it hanging on, in orbit. Then in the 1990s, Jupiter's gravity ripped the comet into pieces.

It was a big comet, and some of the pieces were still 2 km (1¼ miles) across. For two years, the 21 chunks carried on circling Jupiter looking like 21 micro-comets. But then gravity finally sucked them into the planet, destroying the comet totally.

THE PLANET WITH THE STRONGEST GRAVITATIONAL PULL IS JUST A BALL OF GAS

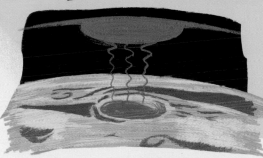

Jupiter is a gas giant, and so has no solid surface—but it has the strongest gravitational force of any planet in the solar system.

If you could visit Jupiter, you would weigh two-and-a-half times as much as you weigh on Earth.

Gravity is the force of attraction between two objects. The more mass an object has, the more gravity acts on it and the more gravitational "pull" of its own it has. Jupiter is the most massive planet in the solar system.

I feel heavy

Me too!

Ceres has been everything— STAR, COMET, PLANET, ASTEROID, and now DWARF PLANET

Ceres is the largest rocky lump in the Asteroid Belt.

It was found in 1801 by an astronomer looking for a star. He thought he'd found a comet, but his friends persuaded him it was a planet.

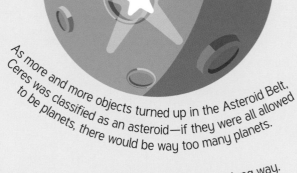

As more and more objects turned up in the Asteroid Belt, Ceres was classified as an asteroid—if they were all allowed to be planets, there would be way too many planets.

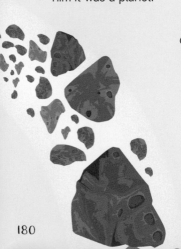

But Ceres is the biggest asteroid by a long way. When the category "dwarf planet" was introduced in 2006, it was reclassified again.

MERCURY COULD SPIN OUT OF CONTROL

Some astronomers think that Jupiter's strong gravity is disrupting the orbit of Mercury.

Mercury already has an odd orbit, and it's vulnerable to being messed about.

There are four possible outcomes, and none looks good for Mercury! Mercury will crash into the Sun; Mercury will be thrown out of the solar system entirely; Mercury will crash into Venus; Mercury will crash into Earth. The last doesn't look good for us, either.

But don't worry—it's not due to happen for 5–7 billion years.

181

CO...ETS GROW A TAIL 'HEN THEY COME NEAR THE SUN

If you see a comet in the sky, it looks spectacular—a bright, shining speck trailing a long glowing tail. But close to, they are messy lumps of rock and dust often shaped like a potato.

Comets orbit the Sun on a long elliptical orbit. As they get close, some of the ice evaporates and the freed gas and dust make up the tail.

The tails always face away from the Sun.

NEARBY COMETS DROP BY EVERY 200 YEARS OR SO

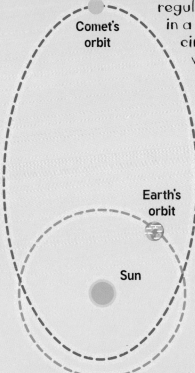

Comet's orbit

Earth's orbit

Sun

Many comets come near Earth regularly. They orbit the Sun in a giant ellipse (squashed circle), and we see them when they come close to Earth in their orbit.

Comets that come back within 200 years are called short-period comets. They spend most of their time in an area called the Kuiper Belt, beyond the orbit of Neptune.

It's a broad band of space 30–55 times as far from the Sun as Earth is, packed with icy lumps. There are trillions of them hanging out there, big and small.

Kuiper Belt

4.5 billion km (2.8 billion miles) to the Sun

THE ICE GIANTS
ARE REALLY VERY HOT

Uranus and Neptune are called ice giants, but the sludgy ice that gives them their name is not cold—it's scalding hot.

Ice is a name for frozen liquids—normal ice is frozen water. But gases can become ice when they are squashed under such immense pressure that the particles don't have room to move around. The temperature is high, but the particles can't move so the "ice" doesn't melt.

Neptune

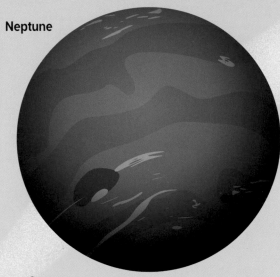

Scientists have made "superionic water ice" by squashing water at pressures two million times Earth's atmosphere. It doesn't melt until it reaches 4,726 °C (8,539 °F)—much hotter than inside the planets.

NEPTUNE AND URANUS ARE SLUDGY SOUP

They're ice planets, but they're not just big chunks of ice.

Uranus

The very top layer is an atmosphere of hydrogen, the same gas as makes up most of Jupiter and Saturn. Below that is a thick layer of water, methane, and ammonia, which probably form sludgy ice. And right in the middle, there is almost certainly a small core of rock and ice.

Atmosphere

Core

Inner mantle

Outer mantle

Methane ice has a blue tinge, and it's methane that means both Neptune and Uranus look blue.

Methane ice is also flammable, so if there were oxygen, the ice giants could burn.

NASA WILL LOOK FOR LIFE IN "OCEAN WORLDS" near the gas giants

Jupiter and Saturn both have moons with vast oceans of water beneath a crust of ice.

Europa (belonging to Jupiter) and Enceladus (belonging to Saturn) are probably the best places to look for life in the solar system beyond Earth.

Enceladus

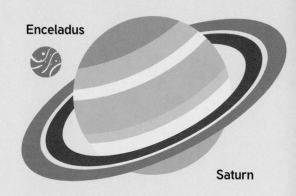

Europa

Saturn

Enceladus has a layer of ice 5 km (3 miles) thick over an ocean 65 km (40 miles) deep. Plumes of water break through the ice near the moon's south pole. Warm water below the surface could be home to microbes, as it is on Earth.

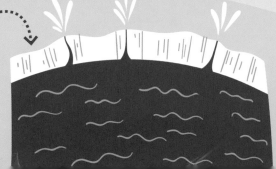

Even our distant ancestors could tell planets from stars

Ancient astronomers thousands of years ago knew there was something different about the planets.

They soon plotted the motion of the planets, and could predict their paths across the sky.

The word "planet" means "wanderer" in Greek. The others were called the "fixed stars."

Both planets and stars just look like spots of bright light if you don't have a telescope. But while the stars stay in the same place in relation to each other night after night and month after month, the planets move among the stars.

COMETS
ARE SNOWBALLS
IN SPACE

A spectacular glowing tail is made by sunlight falling on gas and dust streaming from the comet's body as part of it evaporates in the Sun's heat.

Comets are messy lumps of rock and dust glued together with ice.

The largest known comet, McNaught, is just 25 km (15 miles) wide.

They go around the Sun on a long elliptical orbit.

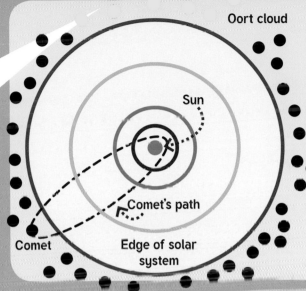

Oort cloud

Sun

Comet's path

Comet

Edge of solar system

Trillions of comets live in the Kuiper Belt, beyond Neptune, and come by the Sun (and us) on orbits shorter than 200 years

Another trillion live further away, in the Oort cloud at the edge of the solar system. Their orbits take thousands or millions of years.

Halley's comet is seen every 76 years. Its tail can be 100 million km (60 million miles) long, but the middle is just 8 km (5 miles) across and 16 km (10 miles) long.

Each pass by the Sun melts some of the comet, so eventually it will be all gone. Halley's comet loses a layer 10 m (33 feet) thick on each visit, so will last another 76,000 years.

A heart-shaped plain on Pluto was probably caused by a comet smashing into the surface, gouging a hole that has filled with frozen nitrogen. It is 1,600 km (1,000 miles) across.

There was a dwarf planet named EASTERBUNNY

—but only until it got its permanent name, Makemake.

It was given the name because it was found just after Easter in 2005.

While the Easter bunny is a rabbit from Western folklore that distributes chocolate eggs, Makemake was the god of fertility in the myths of the Rapanui people of Easter Island. So there's still a connection with Easter.

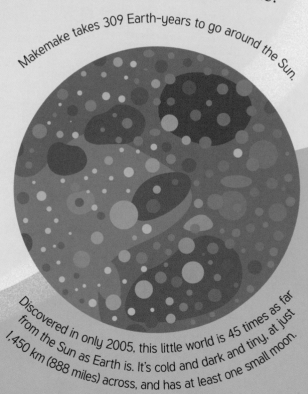

Makemake takes 309 Earth-years to go around the Sun.

Discovered in only 2005, this little world is 45 times as far from the Sun as Earth is. It's cold and dark and tiny, at just 1,450 km (888 miles) across, and has at least one small moon.

PLUTO'S MOONS TUMBLE AROUND RATHER THAN ROTATING SMOOTHLY

The dwarf planet Pluto has at least five moons, of which the smallest, Styx, is only 8 km (5 miles) across at its narrowest.

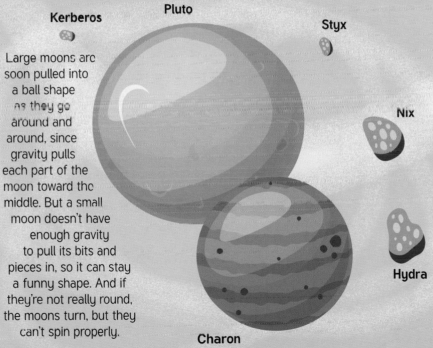

Kerberos

Pluto

Styx

Nix

Hydra

Charon

Large moons are soon pulled into a ball shape as they go around and around, since gravity pulls each part of the moon toward the middle. But a small moon doesn't have enough gravity to pull its bits and pieces in, so it can stay a funny shape. And if they're not really round, the moons turn, but they can't spin properly.

The planets are slowly MOVING AWAY FROM THE SUN

Earth moves away from the Sun at the rate of about 15 cm (6 in) a year.

Scientists aren't sure why. One reason might be that as the Sun gradually uses itself up making heat and light energy, its mass reduces. It then has less gravitational "pull" to hold onto the planets.

The Sun is also slowing down as it spins, which might reduce its ability to keep the planets. The planets themselves slow it down—their gravitational pull has a braking effect on it. Earth reduces the Sun's speed by three milliseconds each century (0.00003 seconds per year).

SATURN TEARS APART BABY MOONS as they form

In Saturn's F ring, tiny moons constantly form and are then destroyed in just a matter of years.

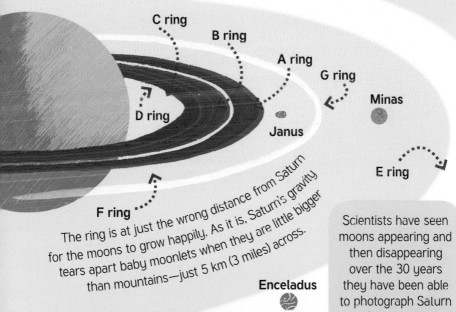

C ring

B ring

A ring

G ring

D ring

Janus

Minas

F ring

E ring

The ring is at just the wrong distance from Saturn for the moons to grow happily. As it is, Saturn's gravity tears apart baby moonlets when they are little bigger than mountains—just 5 km (3 miles) across.

Enceladus

Tethys

Scientists have seen moons appearing and then disappearing over the 30 years they have been able to photograph Saturn from space.

CERES IS JUST A PLANET EMBRYO

It began to form as a planet, but it's too close to Jupiter to grow properly. Scientists call it an embryonic planet.

About 4 billion years ago, Ceres settled into the Asteroid Belt, surrounded by other chunks of left-over material from the start of the solar system.

It makes up a quarter of the mass of the whole Asteroid Belt, but it's only grown to 952 km (592 miles) across. The dwarf planet Pluto is 14 times the mass of tiny Ceres.

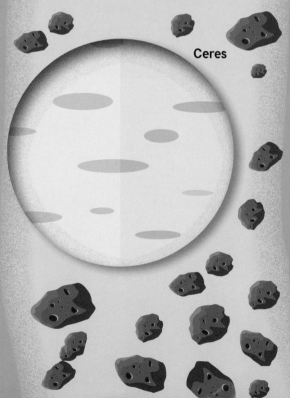

Ceres

PEOPLE USED TO BE TERRIFIED OF COMETS

When Halley's comet was due to be seen in 1910, people panicked and thought it would be the end of the world. Scammers even sold comet-proof hats to stop radiation, and pills to protect people from comet "poison."

In the past, all kinds of disasters were blamed on innocent comets, but they never destroyed the world. But 1910 was the first time scientists could work out that Earth would pass through the comet's tail. People feared it would be poisonous, and possibly wipe out life on Earth. But we're all still here...

Halley's comet has been recorded for more than 2,200 years.

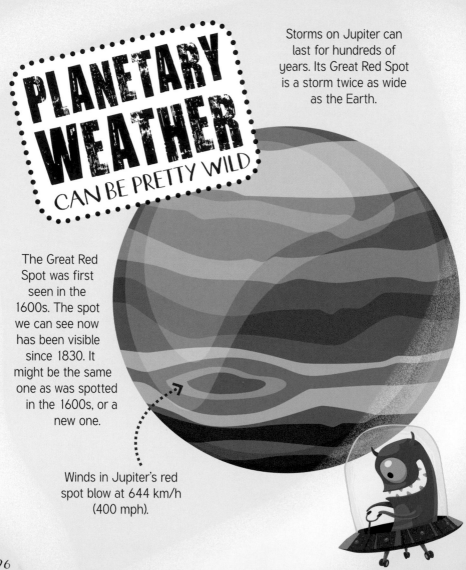

PLANETARY WEATHER
CAN BE PRETTY WILD

Storms on Jupiter can last for hundreds of years. Its Great Red Spot is a storm twice as wide as the Earth.

The Great Red Spot was first seen in the 1600s. The spot we can see now has been visible since 1830. It might be the same one as was spotted in the 1600s, or a new one.

Winds in Jupiter's red spot blow at 644 km/h (400 mph).

The stormiest storm in the solar system is on Neptune. Its Great Dark Spot, seen in 1979, had winds of 2,400 km/h (1,500 mph).

Outside the Spot, winds regularly tear around the planet at nearly 600 m per second (2,000 ft per second).

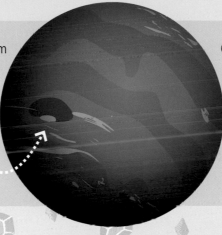

Storms on Neptune and Uranus might produce diamond "hail" from carbon under huge pressure.

The diamond rain could have produced lakes or even oceans of liquid diamond, maybe with floating diamond icebergs.

Venus is the hottest planet in the solar system, with a surface temperature of up to 462 °C (864 °F).

Its atmosphere, made mostly of carbon dioxide, traps heat close to the planet in a runaway greenhouse effect.

Even the clouds are bad on Venus—they're of burning acid that could eat through metal.

SATURN'S FAMOUS RINGS SOMETIMES SEEM TO DISAPPEAR

Saturn and Earth are both tilted on their axis. Every now and then, the tilts mean that the rings around Saturn are edge-on to Earth.

The rings are so thin, top to bottom, that then they seem to disappear completely when seen side-on (but they're still there really).

This was super-confusing for early astronomers. In 1608, the Italian astronomer Galileo first thought Saturn had two very close moons.

But two years later, they had gone. The next time, he saw two half-ellipses with dark triangles between them and the planet—the rings and the gaps between them and Saturn. The rings were not properly explained until 1659.

NEPTUNE AND URANUS HAVE CHANGED PLACES

Some astronomers think Neptune and Uranus formed much closer to the Sun and have moved further out.

Neptune

They also suggest Neptune was originally closer to the Sun than Uranus, but as they moved away from the Sun, Neptune moved further out, swapping places with Uranus.

Uranus

Kuiper belt

The Kuiper Belt, too, was closer to the Sun, near Neptune's current orbit.

199

PLUTO HAS NEARLY AS MUCH LIQUID AS EARTH

If you could collect all the water from Earth and make it into a ball, it would be 692 km (430 miles) across.

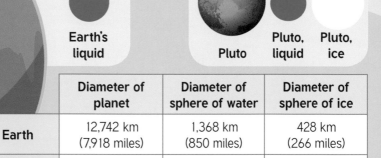

Earth

Earth's liquid

Pluto

Pluto, liquid

Pluto, ice

	Diameter of planet	Diameter of sphere of water	Diameter of sphere of ice
Earth	12,742 km (7,918 miles)	1,368 km (850 miles)	428 km (266 miles)
Pluto	2,377 km (1,477 miles)	1,255 km (780 miles)	1,850 km (1,150 miles)

If you did the same to Pluto, draining its massive sub-surface ocean of water and ammonia, it would make a ball 1,368 km (850 miles) across. And you could make another ice ball from Pluto a massive 1,850 km (1,150 miles) across—bigger than the ball of all Earth's liquid water and ice.

Pluto's huge ocean stretches all around its surface under a thick crust of ice. But it's a poisonous chemical mix that won't be full of Plutonic sea creatures.

THE ASTEROID BELT has been blamed FOR A CRIME IT DIDN'T COMMIT

Rocks from the Moon show evidence of high-energy impacts 4 billion years ago. Scientists blamed a now used-up part of the Asteroid Belt for hurling large rocks around, creating craters on planets and their moons.

But now it seems there were never enough asteroids in the early Asteroid Belt to do all the damage. Instead, lumps and chunks from the early solar system that didn't become part of a planet or moon hurtled around the Sun crashing into things.

201

IS THERE ANOTHER PLANET?

It's possible there is another planet, beyond Neptune and even Pluto.

Planet Nine, NASA suggests, could be 20 times further from the Sun than Neptune. As Neptune is 4.5 billion km (2.8 billion miles) from the Sun, that makes Planet Nine 90 billion km (56 billion miles) away.

The extra planet, sometimes referred to as Planet Nine, is too far away to see with a normal telescope.

Planet Nine is likely to be 10 times the mass of Earth. That's big, but much less massive than the gas giants.

It could take Planet Nine 10,000–20,000 Earth years to orbit the Sun just once.

The gravity of Planet Nine—if it's there—would explain the odd activity of some objects in the Kuiper Belt. Some have a very tilted orbit, move at an angle to the rest of the solar system, or orbit the Sun in the wrong direction.

Planet Nine could be tilting the entire solar system! The planets and other objects don't orbit in line with the Sun's equator, but at an angle of about six degrees.

Planet Nine is likely to be an icy gas planet, like Neptune and Uranus. It would be so far away that it would get very little light or heat from the Sun.

Astronomers are looking for Planet Nine with a huge telescope in Hawaii. It's the best tool we have for finding something small and dark. But they don't even know where to look for it—it could be anywhere in a giant circle around the Sun.

The myth that an extra planet (often called Nibiru) will soon come from the outer edges of the solar system and destroy Earth is an internet hoax, and it's completely false.

Planet Nine might have come from outside the solar system and have been trapped by the Sun's gravity. Or it could have formed with the other planets.

Other stars that have planets often have "super Earths"—planets much larger than Earth but smaller than the gas giants. The Sun notably doesn't have one (unless Planet Nine turns out to be a super Earth!)

The nearest star is
THE SUN

Our Sun is a star like millions of others—it just looks huge and bright because it's so close.

The Sun is a common type of star—it's a medium size, yellow dwarf, main sequence star. That means it's at a healthy stage in the middle of its working life, pumping out energy as heat and light.

The Sun provides all the energy that life on Earth needs. Its gravity keeps Earth and the other planets of the solar system in orbit. We couldn't live without it!

204

IT TAKES EIGHT MINUTES FOR LIGHT TO REACH US FROM THE SUN

Light moves very, very quickly—it covers nearly 400,000 km (186,000 miles) every second. But the Sun is so far away that it still takes 8 minutes and 20 seconds for its light to get to us.

499 light seconds

If the Sun suddenly exploded or went out (don't worry, it won't!), we wouldn't know about it for just over eight minutes.

The time light can travel in an entire year is called a light year. It's nearly 9.5 trillion km (6 trillion miles). That's 9,500,000,000,000 km (6,000,000,000,000 miles).

Astronomers measure distances in space in light years.

KNOW YOUR SUN

Earth would fit inside the Sun 1.3 million times over.

The Sun is 4.6 billion years old.

The Sun weighs 330,000 times as much as Earth.

The Sun spins, turning once on its axis every 27 days.

The Sun is 150 million km (93 million miles) from Earth. That distance is called an astronomical unit (AU).

It would take six months to fly all the way around the Sun in a jumbo jet.

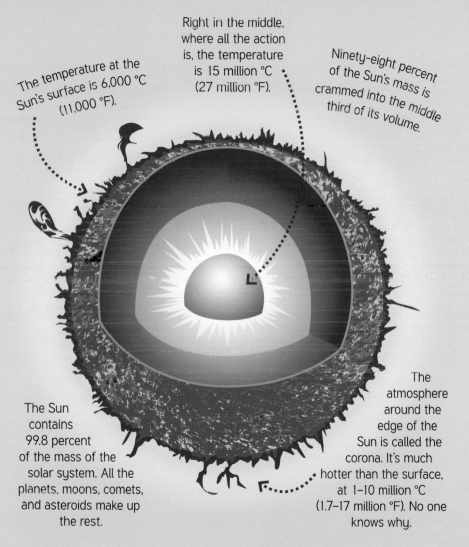

The temperature at the Sun's surface is 6,000 °C (11,000 °F).

Right in the middle, where all the action is, the temperature is 15 million °C (27 million °F).

Ninety-eight percent of the Sun's mass is crammed into the middle third of its volume.

The Sun contains 99.8 percent of the mass of the solar system. All the planets, moons, comets, and asteroids make up the rest.

The atmosphere around the edge of the Sun is called the corona. It's much hotter than the surface, at 1–10 million °C (1.7–17 million °F). No one knows why.

Our next-nearest star is 4.2 light years away—it takes 4.2 years for its light to reach us

But the star is not very bright, so we can't see it at all without a telescope.

After the Sun, the next-nearest star is called Proxima Centauri. It's nearly 40 trillion km (25 trillion miles) away. That's 40,000,000,000,000 km (25,000,000,000,000 miles).

Even in the fastest spacecraft we have, it would take 76,000 years to get Proxima Centauri.

STARS TWINKLE, BUT PLANETS DON'T

The scientific name for the twinkling of stars is "scintillation."

Light from a star

The Earth's atmosphere (with moving pockets of warm and cold air that bounce light around)

Twinkling isn't produced by the stars—it's caused by Earth's atmosphere. Stars are so far away that even through a telescope they're just a bright spot of light.

The light from a single spot is easily bounced around as it passes through the air, seeming to go brighter and dimmer.

A planet is a larger light source because it's closer. Light from different parts is bounced around differently, which cancels out the effect, so planets don't twinkle. If you were up in space, with no atmosphere, the stars wouldn't twinkle.

Nearly every star you can see IS BIGGER THAN THE SUN

Stars come in lots of sizes, but they're a long way away. From Earth, you can only see the biggest and brightest.

There are loads more out there, but most are too faint to see from here.

The Pole star, Polaris, is a bright star in the night sky. It's 2,200 times as bright as the Sun, but so far away it looks like a pinprick.

The Sun is the fourth smallest star we can see from Earth with the naked eye (without a telescope or binoculars). The other three are very faint.

OUR SUN IS ALL ALONE

Many stars have partners; they're part of a system of two, three, or even four stars. These groups of stars all orbit around a single point, which might be empty space.

Our Sun is quite unusual in being just one star on its own. The next star closest to the Sun, Proxima Centauri, is one of three stars that work together.

Systems with more than one star can still have planets. Anything living on one of those planets would be able to look up into the sky and see more than one Sun. They might have more than one sunrise a day!

PEOPLE LONG AGO SAW MANY MORE STARS THAN WE DO

The night sky is not as dark as it used to be.

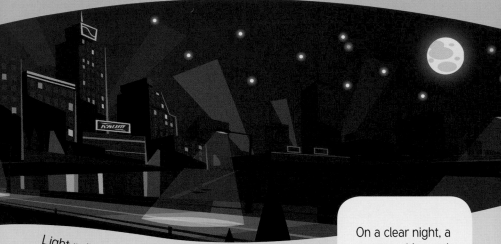

Light pollution is light from street lighting, buildings, and vehicles, which makes the sky lighter at night.

When the sky isn't as dark, faint stars don't show up. Imagine watching fireworks in daylight—it wouldn't be very impressive. It's the same effect. Even a bright full moon hides some of the stars.

On a clear night, a person with good eyesight in a city might see only 100 stars or fewer. In the countryside, they might see 2,500. Centuries ago, a person with good eyes could see 5,000 stars.

Our Sun is a dwarf

All stars are classed as dwarfs, giants, or supergiants.
There's no "normal" stage between dwarf and giant.
Stars are dwarf when they are young and healthy,
working the way a star should work.

They become giant
and then supergiant
when they are old and
wearing out. A star
swells up to a huge
size before it stops
working and dies.

**blue
supergiant**

red giant

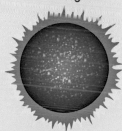

Red and yellow dwarf stars are
doing fine, but a white dwarf has
already died and is much smaller.
It's run out of energy and shrunk
to about the same size as Earth.

white dwarf

**red
dwarf**

**sun-like star/
yellow dwarf**

Red-hot stars are
THE COOLEST

We're used to thinking of red things as super-hot,
but that's only because we link fire and heat with red.

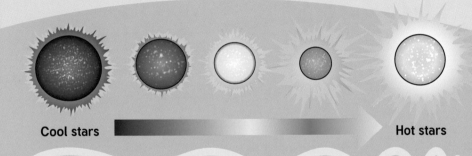

Cool stars   **Hot stars**

Long wavelengths   **Short wavelengths**

As things get hotter,
they throw out light at
different wavelengths,
which we see as
different shades.

Red is the first type of light to shine out as something
gets hot, so it comes from the coolest hot things.

The hottest stars shine with pale blue light—but we
think of blue things as cold! Between red and blue,
stars glow yellow, orange, and white.

THE SUN IS GREEN

All stars push out light in all wavelengths, but more of one wavelength than others, depending on how hot they are.

As a yellow dwarf, our Sun is pretty hot, and pours out a lot of green light. But green is in the middle of the range we can see (the spectrum) and our eyes mix it with the other wavelengths the Sun pushes out, so it ends up looking white.

Sometimes at an eclipse, it's just possible to see a greenish tinge around the Sun.

There are other green stars out there, too, and they all look white to us.

SMALL STARS GO SLOWLY AND STEADILY

The smallest healthy stars are called red dwarfs. The biggest are just half the size of our Sun. The smallest are less than a tenth the size of the Sun, at 7.5 percent of its mass.

Red dwarfs use up their hydrogen so slowly that they produce energy at 1/10,000th the rate of the Sun. They can keep going for 10 trillion years— about 1,000 times as long as the universe has existed. That means every single red dwarf is still right at the start of its life.

MOST STARS ARE HARD TO SEE EVEN WITH THE BEST TELESCOPES

Red dwarfs are the smallest and dimmest active stars.

Between two-thirds and three-quarters of all stars are red dwarfs, and we can't see most of them, so we don't know exactly how many there are.

With good telescopes sited in space, astronomers can see red dwarfs that are fairly nearby, in our part of the galaxy. But no one can see those that are further away.

They're very dim because they release energy very slowly. That means if they have planets, they will have to stay close to the star to be warm enough for liquid water and possible life.

STARS ARE ENERGY FACTORIES

Stars like the Sun make energy by messing about with matter in a way that's called "nuclear fusion."

All stars are mostly hydrogen gas, one of the two chemical elements that were created at the Big Bang (see page 252).

At the middle of a star, hydrogen is squashed together under such huge pressure it becomes another gas, called helium.

It takes four atoms of hydrogen to make one atom of helium, but not absolutely everything is used up. The last tiny bit escapes as energy.

Although each reaction is tiny, there's enough helium-making going on to release all the light and heat of a star.

p p
p p
4 x hydrogen

→

n p n
p
helium

+

energy

p = **proton**

n = **neutron**

Stars keep going until they've used up a lot of their hydrogen.

Before they die, they start making different chemicals by fusing the helium.

When large stars explode (see page 227), iron fuses in the explosion, making all the other elements in the universe.

All the elements made in the stars are scattered when a star explodes.

HUGE STARS ARE FAST AND FURIOUS

The biggest stars of all are supergiants. Their mass can be 100 times the mass of the Sun, and they are hundreds of times as far across as the Sun.

Supergiants produce energy at an astonishing rate. They can produce 100,000 times as much energy as the Sun, so shine 100,000 times brighter.

Even though they are big, they whizz through their fuel supply quickly. They last only a few million years before their fuel is all used up.

Betelgeuse in the Orion constellation is 700 times as wide as the Sun

Orion constellation

THE SUN IS LOSING WEIGHT
(Well, mass)

As the Sun pumps out energy, it uses up some of its mass.

In fact, it loses about 4,400 million kg (4 million tons) of its mass in nuclear fusion every second. That means it gets slimmer by the mass of the Earth every 47 million years.

It sounds alarming—that's a lot. But not for the Sun.

Its current mass is about 2,000,000,000,000,000,000,000,000,000,000 kg (2,200,000,000,000,000,000,000,000,000 tons). By the end of its life, in around 5 billion years, it will have lost only 0.034 percent of its current mass.

THE SUN HAS A PROBLEM WITH SPOTS

Sunspots are dark patches on the surface of the Sun. They're not really dark—they just look dark by comparison with the super-bright areas around them.

Sunspots are cooler than the rest of the Sun's surface. But they're still pretty hot at 4,200 °C (7,700 °F) instead of 6,000 °C (11,000 °F).

They're not small spots—they can be 160,000 km (100,000 miles) across. That's 12 times as wide as the Earth.

PEOPLE HAVE ALWAYS SEEN PICTURES IN THE STARS

They're called constellations or asterisms. Some were first named 3,000 years ago in Mesopotamia (ancient Iraq).

People see different things in the stars. Ursa Major was seen as a bear in Ancient Greece and a wagon in Mesopotamia.

In Burma, it's a prawn or crab, and an Arab story describes it as a coffin followed by three mourners.

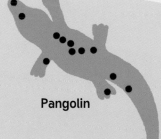

Pangolin

When Europeans started sailing south and saw unfamiliar stars, they invented new pictures, including "electric machine," "earthworm," "pangolin," and "slug."

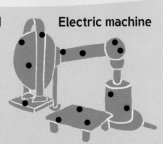

Electric machine

SOMETIMES STARS GO WALKABOUT

Not all stars are stuck in place with their band of planets; some wander around.

A red dwarf called Scholz's star drifted through the outer edge of our solar system 70,000 years ago.

Saturn

Scholz's star

Uranus

Pluto

Two more stars will pass by, but not too soon. One called Hip 85605 will visit in 240,000–470,000 years, and another called GL710 will drop by in about 1.3 million years.

Sun

Oort Cloud

They will pass through the Oort Cloud, far from the Sun. They'll only cause problems if they push objects out of the Oort Cloud and onto a collision course with us, which isn't likely.

THE SUN HAS LAYERS, LIKE AN ONION

The inside of the Sun has three main layers—the core, where the work happens; the radiative zone, where energy moves slowly to the surface; and the convective zone, where it moves around in currents.

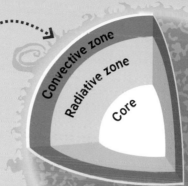

Convective zone

Radiative zone

Core

Corona

Chromosphere

Core

Photosphere

Convective zone

Radiative zone

The convective zone brings energy to the surface, called the photosphere. Beyond that are the layers of the Sun's atmosphere—the chromosphere and then the corona.

THE FATE OF A STAR DEPENDS ON ITS SIZE

1 As stars use up their hydrogen fuel, they swell up.

2 A star the size of the Sun turns first to a red giant. It can be millions of miles across.

3 When the red giant wears out, the outer layers puff out and the middle collapses into itself, becoming a super-dense white dwarf.

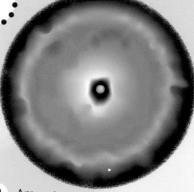

4 Around 98 percent of stars become white dwarfs.

5 Over trillions of years, a white dwarf cools to a black dwarf, an invisible, cold black blob in the dark sky.

Just a teaspoon of white-dwarf material could weigh 13.5 tonnes (15 tons).

Stars more than eight times the mass of the Sun explode in a spectacular supernova.

The last supernova seen clearly from Earth happened in 1604.

A large star first becomes a red giant or supergiant, then after a few million years it blows apart.

The explosion lasts a week or more, shining more brightly than any star in the sky.

Neutron star

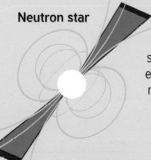

The leftovers from a supernova are a cloud of expanding gas and, in the middle, a neutron star or a black hole.

Black hole

THE SUN WILL DIE IN AROUND 5 BILLION YEARS

It won't go with a bang—it's too small for that. When it runs out of hydrogen it can use, the Sun will swell to a red giant, taking in Mercury and Venus.

The surface will be uncomfortably close to Earth.

Then it will lose its outer layers, leaving a hard, dense white dwarf about the size of the Earth— but still with much of its mass.

Gravity at the surface will be 100,000 times Earth's gravity, and it will be 20 times as hot as the Sun's outer parts are now. Heat escapes slowly into space, so it will take trillions of years to turn into a cold, dead black dwarf.

It takes light
A MILLION YEARS TO
GET OUT OF THE SUN

Light is produced as photons (packets of energy) deep in the Sun. But the Sun is very dense and it takes a very long time for a photon to get out.

Each photon is taken in and kicked out again by one particle after another. It's not heading in any particular direction; it bumbles around randomly.

Inside, the Sun is opaque—the opposite of transparent. It's about as opaque as a rock, so it takes a long time for light to move through it.

A single photon can spend up to 170,000 years wandering from the middle to the surface.

INSIDE A SUPERNOVA, a star collapses to a ball 10 km (6 miles) across

The largest stars fuse elements up to iron and can then go no further. The core collapses and the energy is so intense it blows the star apart.

Only a tiny, dense middle is left and the rest is scattered.

The gravity in the core of a collapsed star is so great that all the space is crushed out of it and it becomes solid matter.

If the core is 1.4 to 5 times the mass of the Sun, it becomes a neutron star. If it has more mass than that, it becomes a black hole.

A teaspoonful of neutron star would weigh TENS OF MILLIONS OF TONS

All the space has been squeezed out of a neutron star, leaving only the heavy bits of matter crushed together. There's not even space within the atoms.

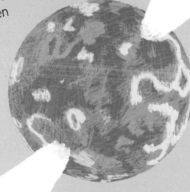

A neutron star with three times the mass of the Sun might be just the size of a small city, but it still has almost the same mass it had as a giant star.

Neutron stars spin around super-fast—hundreds of times each second.

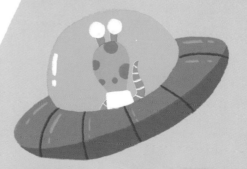

THE SURFACE OF THE SUN ISN'T A SURFACE AT ALL

Photosphere

Sunspots

The Sun has no surface—it's a giant ball of super-squashed gas. The part we call the surface is just the point we can't see past, but it wouldn't be solid to stand on.

The lowest level of the Sun's atmosphere we can see is called the photosphere and treated as the surface. Sunspots appear on the photosphere.

Close up, it looks bubbly, like a pot of boiling water. It's constantly moving and changing. The "surface" of any star would look much the same.

THERE ARE 100 MILLION NEUTRON STARS IN THE MILKY WAY

Some are impossible to see because they don't push out any light, but the number can be worked out from how many stars should have gone supernova by now.

A neutron star is not still making energy, but its surface can be scorching hot: 600,000 °C (1,100,000 °F).

I feel so flat!

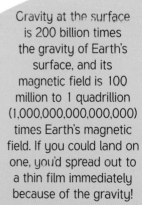

Gravity at the surface is 200 billion times the gravity of Earth's surface, and its magnetic field is 100 million to 1 quadrillion (1,000,000,000,000,000) times Earth's magnetic field. If you could land on one, you'd spread out to a thin film immediately because of the gravity!

THE SOLAR WIND IS HOT AND VERY WINDY

Solar wind comes from the Sun, blowing into space. It's a stream of charged particles, such as electrons and photons, that pours from the Sun's corona all the time as the corona expands into space.

The solar wind is not like any wind on Earth— it "blows" at 900 km (560 miles) per second and is 1,000,000 °C (1,800,000 °F). It's the solar wind that blows the tail of a comet, carrying it away from the Sun. That's why a comet's tail always points away from the Sun, whichever way the comet is moving.

Stars are born in vast star nurseries

Huge clouds of dust and gas gather together and collapse to form stars. As the cloud makes clumps, each clump has its own gravity, and that draws it closer together.

All stars start with the same ingredients—about three-quarters hydrogen to one quarter helium, mixed with a small amount of other chemicals.

During the course of the star's life, the proportions change as hydrogen is used up and made into helium. So hydrogen decreases and helium increases.

It gets ever more dense, drawing in toward its middle, until each clump starts to fuse hydrogen, becoming a star.

THE BIGGEST STARS ARE 1,700 TIMES THE SIZE OF THE SUN

It's hard to say exactly which star is the largest. One contender for the title is NML Cygni, 5,300 light years away. It could be anywhere between 1,642 and 2,775 times as wide as the Sun.

If we assume it's somewhere in the middle, and put it where the Sun is, everything out to the orbit of Uranus would be swallowed up in the star.

The brightest star is called Pistol. It shines up to 10 million times as brightly as the Sun. So much radiation comes from it, that even if it has any planets they could not support life.

THE BRIGHTEST STARS ARE NOT THE CLOSEST

Long ago, people thought all stars were the same distance from Earth, as though they were painted on the inside of an upturned bowl.

Now we know that they stretch backward into space and are all at different distances from us.

It's impossible to tell whether a star is near or far from how brightly it shines. It could be small and dim but close, or big and bright but a long way off.

I definitely look brightest from Earth!

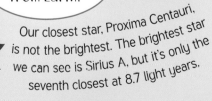

Our closest star, Proxima Centauri, is not the brightest. The brightest star we can see is Sirius A, but it's only the seventh closest at 8.7 light years.

ALL THE STARS YOU CAN SEE ARE IN THE MILKY WAY

The Milky Way is only one of at least 100 billion galaxies in the universe, all packed with their own stars.

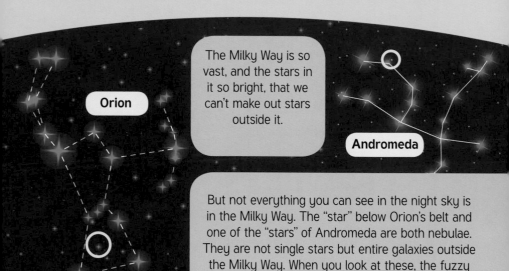

The Milky Way is so vast, and the stars in it so bright, that we can't make out stars outside it.

Orion

Andromeda

But not everything you can see in the night sky is in the Milky Way. The "star" below Orion's belt and one of the "stars" of Andromeda are both nebulae. They are not single stars but entire galaxies outside the Milky Way. When you look at these, the fuzzy cloud of light you see is collected from hundreds of billions of stars.

Andromeda is the closest galaxy, 2.5 million light years away.

THE SUN HAS A SPIKY OVERCOAT

The Sun has a layer above the surface called the chromosphere, which has spiky structures called spicules.

The spikes are 500–1,000 km (300–600 miles) across and grow up to 10,000 km (6,000 miles) long before they collapse.

Spicules are jets of plasma that burst from the surface at 96 km (60 miles) per second—more than 320,000 km/h (200,000 mph). Each lasts just 5–10 minutes. There are about 10 million spicules at any time.

THE SUN WAS MUCH FAINTER WHEN IT WAS YOUNG

Stars like the Sun grow brighter as they get older. The Sun would have had only 70 percent of its current brightness when it was shiny and new.

But that doesn't work with what we know of conditions on Earth and Mars. If the Sun was putting out about a third less energy, Earth and Mars should have been too cold for liquid water—but they weren't. Both had lots of water in the distant past.

Early Earth

Early Mars

Yes, commander, water has been spotted on Earth and Mars...

Earth certainly had water when life first appeared, about 4 billion years ago. It's a puzzle no one has managed to solve so far.

THE STARS ARE SLOWLY MOVING IN DIFFERENT DIRECTIONS

The stars seem to move all together in a circle during a night, but that's because Earth is turning.

They are actually all moving separately. Some are moving away from Earth, some are moving toward Earth, and they are moving relative to each other.

The stars closest to us seem to move most, because the same amount of change looks larger.

The first person to notice their genuine movement was Edmund Halley. In 1718, he noticed that the positions of some stars had moved since the Ancient Greeks described them. But only a tiny bit, in 2,000 years!

Seven baby stars will be BORN THIS YEAR

And that's just in the Milky Way.

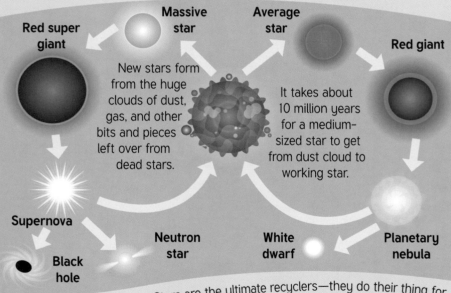

Red super giant

Massive star

Average star

Red giant

New stars form from the huge clouds of dust, gas, and other bits and pieces left over from dead stars.

It takes about 10 million years for a medium-sized star to get from dust cloud to working star.

Supernova

Black hole

Neutron star

White dwarf

Planetary nebula

New stars are being created all the time.

Stars are the ultimate recyclers—they do their thing for a few billion years, making and managing their system of planets, and then they wind up the whole show and the bits can be reused. Some go out with a bang—a really, really big bang.

242

THE SUN HAS MEGA-TORNADOES

Up to 11,000 massive tornadoes rage through the atmosphere of the Sun at any one time. They help whip up the temperature, making the corona super-hot.

As well as normal solar flares, there are nanoflares. They have only a billionth of the energy of a regular flare—but each one is still the equivalent of a ten megaton hydrogen bomb. And there are millions every second.

Explosions add to the heat and chaos.

BABY STARS GROW SLOWLY

It took 10 million years for our Sun to grow from a cloud of dust and gas. But then it will live for 10,000 million years— 1,000 times as long as it took to grow.

Some stars grow much more quickly. A few even take just 75,000 years.

I am the biggest star around here!

Yes, but I'll get to be much older.

It's not small stars that grow quickly, but really big ones. So small stars grow slowly and have a long and leisurely life, while big stars grow fast, live life in the fast lane, and die young.

THE MILKY WAY IS ON A COLLISION COURSE

The Milky Way and the galaxy closest to it, the Andromeda Galaxy, are heading for a crash.

Andromeda is moving toward us at 110 km (68 miles) per second; the collision is due in about 4 billion years.

There's lots of space between stars, so it will probably be a largely peaceful merger with very few stars actually colliding.

It could be a three-way crash, as the Triangulum, the third largest galaxy in the Local Group, is moving in the same direction. The new, combined galaxy has already been named: Milkdromeda, or Milkomeda.

THE STARS ARE STILL THERE IN THE DAYTIME

But we can't see them because the Sun is so bright they don't show up.

Photos taken from the Moon show a sky with no stars in. That's because the Earth is so close, and reflects so much light from the Sun, that it swamps the light of the stars.

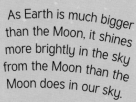

As Earth is much bigger than the Moon, it shines more brightly in the sky from the Moon than the Moon does in our sky.

In space, astronauts looking away from the Sun, Earth, and Moon can see more stars because there is no atmosphere to absorb any of their light.

The stars in a constellation can be FURTHER FROM EACH OTHER than from us

Although the stars in a constellation look close together in the sky, they are not actually near each other in space.

Space is three-dimensional, so some stars can be further back (so further from Earth) than others. There's nothing in space to give us any idea of depth.

Alkaid
210 light years

For example, in the constellation Ursa Major, the star Dubhe is 123 light years away from us, while the star Merak is 78 light years away.

Dubhe
123 light years

Phecda
90 light years

Mizar
88 light years

Alioth
68 light years

Merak
78 light years

The stars move independently, so over a long time the constellations drift out of shape. In 100,000 years, the Southern Cross will be two parallel lines!

Megrez
63 light years

BROWN DWARFS DON'T MAKE IT AS STARS

They're between super-sized planets and tiny stars, but are just too small to work as stars.

They have between twice the mass of Jupiter and just under a tenth the mass of the Sun.

Brown dwarfs are very hard to see, as they don't produce much light. They show up with infrared telescopes, though.

It's not enough to kick-start the nuclear fusion that powers stars. But neither are they quite a planet, as they're too big for that.

There might be as many brown dwarfs as there are proper, working stars.

SOME STARS ARE NO WARMER THAN YOUR BODY

Y-dwarfs are the coldest type of star—or nearly star.
They are the coolest brown dwarfs.

Although at the start of their lives, brown dwarfs might have just enough mass to do a tiny bit of fusion, they stop after a few million years and the only heat they produce comes from shrinking because of their gravity.

There are three classes of brown dwarf.

It's summer on Earth—I want to go home.

We could stop by that brown dwarf if you want a day in the Sun?

The surface of the hottest brown dwarf could be 750 °C (1,380 °F), but the coolest are just 25 °C (80 °F). That's the temperature of a nice day on Earth.

MILKY WAY

The Milky Way is a disk 100,000 light years across—but only 1,000 light years thick.

The Milky Way is a spiral galaxy. That means it's got a whirling-round shape, with arms trailing out into space.

There are four main arms and some smaller arms. We are on a smaller arm, 28,000 light years from the middle.

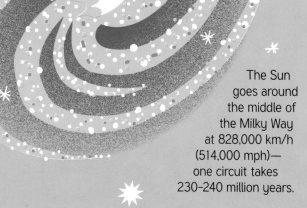

If the solar system out to Neptune's orbit was 2.5 cm (1 in) across, the Milky Way would be as wide as the USA.

The Sun goes around the middle of the Milky Way at 828,000 km/h (514,000 mph)— one circuit takes 230–240 million years.

There are up to 400 billion stars in the Milky Way.

No one knew the Milky Way was a massive band of stars until 1610 when it was first seen through a telescope.

The Milky Way is part of a group of galaxies called, unimaginatively, the Local Group.

Between 1 billion and 1 trillion years from now, the Milky Way and all the other galaxies of the Local Group will have merged into a single mega-galaxy.

Two dwarf galaxies are merging with the Milky Way right now, but they don't affect us.

There is probably a supermassive black hole at the middle of the Milky Way.

THE UNIVERSE STARTED WITH A BANG

The start of the universe is called the Big Bang.

One second

Three minutes

The first bits of matter—nuclei, the middles of atoms—appeared in the first minutes. This was almost all hydrogen and helium.

The Big Bang was silent—there was no "bang."

There was no explosion to see, either—even if there had been anything with eyes to see it.

Everything expanded from a tiny point to the size of a grapefruit in just 0.0000000000000 000000000000000001 second.

In this time, the universe doubled in size 90 times.

All space, time, matter, and energy in the universe were created in an instant.

Light first emerged from the darkness after 380,000 years— astronomers can still trace some of it.

380,000 years

1 billion years

15 billion years

By this point, clouds of matter clumped into lumps that became galaxies and stars and planets.

No one knows what, if anything, existed before the Big Bang, or is outside the universe. "Before" and "outside" might be meaningless.

Atoms formed as nuclei combined with electrons

Galaxies have different shapes, but lots are spirals with "arms" made by their whirling motion in space.

The hydrogen and helium created in the first minutes still power the stars.

When we look into space, WE SEE THE PAST

Light takes a very, very long time to reach us from distant objects in the sky. If a star is 50,000 light years away, the light we see when we look at the night sky left the star 50,000 years ago.

The North star, Polaris, is 323 light years away, so we see it as it was 323 years ago. If it had exploded in 1900, we wouldn't see the explosion until around 200 years from now.

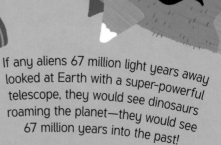

If any aliens 67 million light years away looked at Earth with a super-powerful telescope, they would see dinosaurs roaming the planet—they would see 67 million years into the past!

THE UNIVERSE WILL HAVE A BIG BIRTHDAY IN 200 MILLION YEARS

The universe is about 13.8 billion years old, so it will be 14 billion in just 200 million years.

The first stars probably appeared around 180 million years after the Big Bang. They were the first lights in a previously pitch-black universe.

None of those stars still exists, but the light from them is still crossing the universe, so we can see them in the past.

255

THE UNIVERSE IS STILL GETTING BIGGER

The Big Bang was the sudden appearance of everywhere (all space-time), but then "everywhere" got bigger.

It didn't expand into empty space but space appeared in between the stuff of the universe, pushing it apart.

If you drew stars on a balloon and blew up the balloon, you would see the same effect—the stars would get further apart.

Around 5-6 billion years after the Big Bang, the speed at which the universe was growing bigger increased. So it got bigger more quickly, and is still getting bigger, faster and faster.

If the universe had kept expanding at the same rate (following the red line), it wouldn't be as big as it is now.

Big Bang

5-6 billion years

The Hubble Space Telescope CAN SEE DISTANT GALAXIES, but not Pluto

Hubble can show fantastic detail in a galaxy 72 million light years away, but Pluto look likes a blurry blob in Hubble photos.

How much Hubble can see depends on the size of the object, how much light it produces, and how far away it is. A galaxy 50,000 light years across is 4 billion times the size of Pluto. It's packed with stars pumping out light, but Pluto just reflects the light of the Sun from its tiny area.

Pluto

At its closest, Pluto is about 5 light-hours from Earth. The galaxy is 74 billion times further away than Pluto.

distant galaxy

ONLY ONE SUPERNOVA HAS BEEN OBSERVED IN REAL TIME

In 2008, a NASA astronomer just happened to be looking at the right bit of space to see a star explode in a supernova at that very moment.

Though it's not quite "at that very moment," because it actually happened 88 million years ago.

The star-stuff exploded outward at 10,000 km (6,200 miles) per second—that's nearly 36 million km/h (23 million mph).

Catching the first five minutes of a supernova means astronomers now know what to look for and hope to spot hundreds every year.

WE ARE RIGHT IN THE MIDDLE OF THE OBSERVABLE UNIVERSE

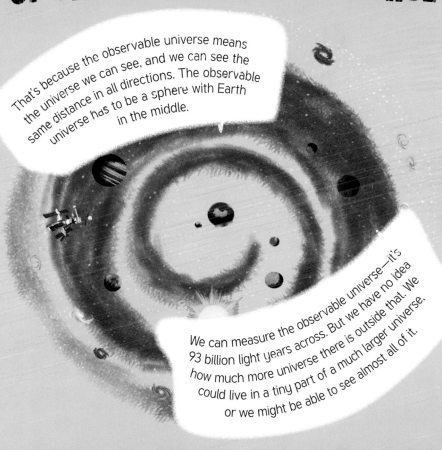

That's because the observable universe means the universe we can see, and we can see the same distance in all directions. The observable universe has to be a sphere with Earth in the middle.

We can measure the observable universe—it's 93 billion light years across. But we have no idea how much more universe there is outside that. We could live in a tiny part of a much larger universe, or we might be able to see almost all of it.

BLACK HOLES AREN'T HOLES AT ALL

Holes are gaps where there's nothing. A hole in your pocket is where there's no pocket and things can fall through. But a black hole is somewhere that has more stuff, not less.

It's an area where matter is so squashed there is no space in it at all, not even within the atoms.

It won't stop pulling me!

Gravity is produced by objects with mass, and as a black hole has a lot of mass it has a lot of gravity.

Anything that gets too close to a black hole is pulled toward it and squashed along with everything else. That's how black holes grow.

THERE'S A BLACK HOLE
at the middle of the Milky Way

The galaxy has a supermassive black hole in the middle.
It has the mass of four million Suns and is called
Sagittarius A* (pronounced "A-star").

In fact, there are probably two, the second one having the mass of only 100,000 Suns. These are just the big ones—there are more than 100 million smaller black holes in the Milky Way.

Steer well clear of the middle, captain!

All galaxies probably have a huge black hole in the middle, with the mass of millions or billions of stars crushed into a small space. As they take in more dust, gas, and other matter all the time, they grow ever larger.

IF THE SUN TURNED TO A BLACK HOLE, Earth wouldn't be pulled into it

(But we would have other problems! Don't worry, it can't happen.)

The edge of a black hole is called its event horizon. That's the point at which it's no longer possible to escape being pulled in. You'd need to be just 10 km (6 miles) from the Sun-as-black-hole to be pulled into it.

Event horizon

How far the event horizon is from the surface depends on the mass of the black hole. The black hole has the same gravity as a star of the same mass, so if you were a safe distance from the star, you're still a safe distance from the black hole.

THE FLASH OF THE BIG BANG WAS DELAYED BY 378,000 YEARS

Although there was no big flash at the time of the Big Bang, a massive radiation burst was freed 380,000 years later.

Until then photons (particles of energy) just bumbled around in random directions. When conditions changed, they could move in straight lines and start spreading out at the speed of light—in a flash of microwaves, not visible light. It's called the cosmic microwave background radiation (CMBR).

Big bang

Photons

CMBR

We can't see back before 380,000 years ago, just like we can't see through the clouds—the universe was opaque before then.

263

ASTRONOMERS SPOT BLACK HOLES BY WATCHING THINGS GO AROUND NOTHING

It's impossible to see a black hole in black space— it looks like nothing.

Although we can't see black holes with telescopes, there are giveaway signs that they are there.

Where stars or other objects seem to go around an empty patch of sky, there might be a black hole lurking there.

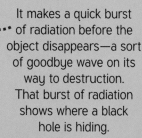

Matter pulled into a black hole goes faster and faster. This creates friction with the stuff around it.

It makes a quick burst of radiation before the object disappears—a sort of goodbye wave on its way to destruction. That burst of radiation shows where a black hole is hiding.

The first radio waves from space
WERE MISTAKEN FOR PIGEONS

In 1964, two radio engineers tried to track down a problem with radio signals.

They thought it was a technical fault or interference. And then they thought it was caused by pigeons nesting inside their equipment. They cleared out the pigeons, but the signal still came. At last they realized the "hiss" they had found was the echo of the Big Bang—cosmic microwave background radiation.

The pigeon trap they used to catch the birds is on display in the Smithsonian Air and Space Museum in Washington, DC, USA.

Black holes come in three sizes—tiny, small, and huge

Tiny black holes are the size of an atom or smaller.

Small black holes are created after huge stars collapse in a supernova explosion.

And supermassive giant black holes exist in the middle of galaxies. They can be billions of times larger than the small black holes.

There don't seem to be medium-sized black holes, though. They could be at the heart of dwarf galaxies—but dwarf galaxies are hard to see as they're faint and distant. Or there might really not be any medium-sized black holes.

THE UNIVERSE COULD END WITH A BANG OR A WHIMPER

The universe is still expanding, getting more and more spread out. Where will it end? No one knows for sure.

The universe could carry on getting bigger quickly until it's just a thin, dark soup of matter where nothing can hold itself together—a Big Rip.

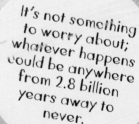

It's not something to worry about; whatever happens could be anywhere from 2.8 billion years away to never.

Or it could reach a final size where matter is so far apart that there is no movement or heat. Or everything could bounce back toward the middle in a reverse of the Big Bang—a Big Crunch.

THE UNIVERSE MIGHT BE BOUNCY

If the universe started as a tiny point, is now expanding, and then will shrink back to a tiny point, it could do this again and again in a sequence of "Big Bounces."

That would mean our "turn" in the universe is just one of many. Space, time, matter, and the laws of physics might all be completely different in other "bounces."

Another Big Bang—the cycle repeats

Big Bang

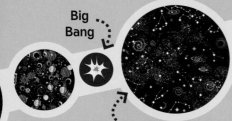

Universe rushing inward

Normal universe

The universe could even turn inside out when it all shrinks back together. The last bit of shrinking, with gravity pulling everything into nothing, would be super-quick, just as the first expansion was super-quick.

WE SENT A RADIO MESSAGE
TO ALIENS

In 1974, astronomers in Puerto Rico beamed a radio message toward a group of stars huddled at the edge of the Milky Way.

This cosmic "hello" thrown out into the universe carried a set of simple pictures intended to tell aliens we exist. It was the most powerful radio signal ever transmitted.

The bunch of 300,000 stars is called M13. It's 21,000 light years away, so even if anyone picks it up, we won't get an answer for 42,000 years. It was broadcast just once, for three minutes, so let's hope the aliens were paying attention.

EXOPLANETS ARE PLANETS AROUND OTHER STARS

The earliest evidence of exoplanets is a photo taken in 1917, but its significance wasn't noticed for 90 years.

Telescopes in space such as Kepler and the planned James Webb telescope look for exoplanets that might have the right conditions for life.

There are probably more than a trillion planets outside our galaxy.

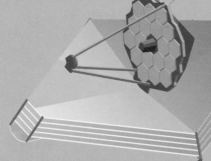

Around four thousand exoplanets have been found so far.

Exoplanets include rocky planets, ice or ocean planets, cold gassy planets, hot gassy planets, and "lava worlds."

Exoplanet 55 Cancri is half solid and half molten.

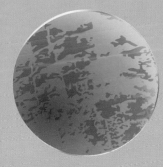

Most exoplanets are gas planets, like Jupiter and Saturn.

Proxima Centauri, our nearest star, has an exoplanet only 4.2 light years from us.

The most massive exoplanet ever found is called HR 2562 b. It's 30 times the mass of Jupiter, which might be too big for a planet—it could be a brown dwarf instead.

Exoplanets' "years" range from a few hours to thousands of Earth years.

Ooh, it's my birthday again!

OUR SOLAR SYSTEM HAS BEEN VISITED BY AN OBJECT FROM OUTSIDE

Late in 2017, an asteroid from another star system in the Milky Way whizzed into our solar system, looped round the Sun, and left again.

The splinter of rock 230 m (800 ft) long and 35 m (100 ft) wide was named Oumuamua from the Hawaiian for "scout."

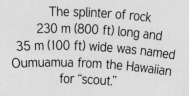

No one noticed it until it had already zipped past Mars, Earth, Mercury, and Venus, gone around the back of the Sun, and was heading away again.

The International Astronomical Union invented a new classification for asteroids from far away; Oumuamua is 1I (I for "interstellar").

We can spot planets around other stars by seeing the stars go dim

As a planet passes in front of a star, it blocks a little bit of the light from the star—just as if you hold your hand up in front of a light bulb.

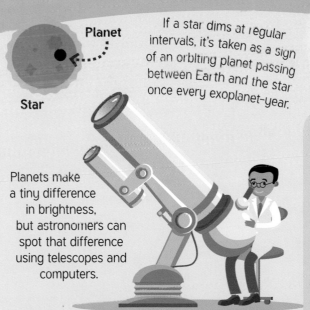

Planet

Star

If a star dims at regular intervals, it's taken as a sign of an orbiting planet passing between Earth and the star once every exoplanet-year.

Planets make a tiny difference in brightness, but astronomers can spot that difference using telescopes and computers.

Only planets on a direct line between Earth and their star will show up. If a planet's too high or low to block light from Earth, we won't know it's there. Only one in 100 exoplanets can be found; the rest stay hidden.

273

IF EARTH IS DESTROYED BY AN ASTEROID, WE MIGHT NOT SEE IT COMING

What is the chance of this happening in the next few hundreds of years? Zero.

If we saw an asteroid coming, we might even be able to knock it off course or blow it up. But if it was dark, and came sneakily fast with the Sun behind it, or from outside the solar system, it could be here with no warning.

A medium-sized asteroid slipped between Earth and the Moon in January 2017. Astronomers didn't spot it until two days before. If it had hit, it would have made an explosion 35 times as large as an atomic bomb.

IT'S VERY, VERY COLD IN SPACE

The temperature in deep space is about -270.5 °C (-455 °F).

That's only a few degrees warmer than the coldest temperature that is possible anywhere, -273.15 °C (-459.7 °F). At that point, all the particles in matter stop moving—nothing can be colder.

Quick! Its much warmer by that star!

Not all space is freezing, though. Gas between stars, or the solar wind (stream of particles) from stars, can be very hot, reaching thousands or even millions of degrees.

It's warmer the closer you get to a star. A thermometer in space above Earth, half in the sun and half in shade, would show about 7 °C (45 °F).

BLACK HOLES COULD BE TUNNELS TO WHITE HOLES

Most astronomers think matter that gets pulled into a black hole is compressed and destroyed. But a few think black holes are tunnels to another universe.

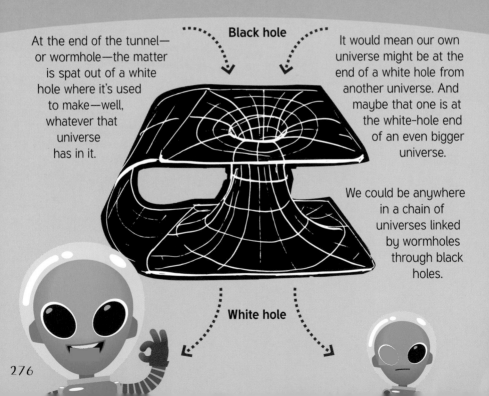

Black hole

At the end of the tunnel—or wormhole—the matter is spat out of a white hole where it's used to make—well, whatever that universe has in it.

It would mean our own universe might be at the end of a white hole from another universe. And maybe that one is at the white-hole end of an even bigger universe.

We could be anywhere in a chain of universes linked by wormholes through black holes.

White hole

THE GALAXY IS HURTLING TOWARD A MYSTERIOUS OBJECT

The Earth moves round the Sun,
the Sun moves around the galaxy, and the Milky Way, along
with the other galaxies in its supercluster, moves toward
something called the Great Attractor.

No one really knows what it is, but it's
500 million light years across and has a mass
1,000 trillion (1,000,000,000,000,000) times
the mass of the Sun.

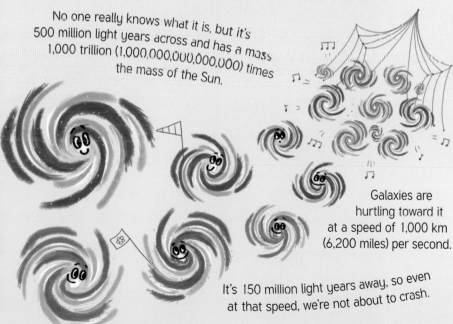

Galaxies are
hurtling toward it
at a speed of 1,000 km
(6,200 miles) per second.

It's 150 million light years away, so even
at that speed, we're not about to crash.

THE UNIVERSE LOOKS LIKE A GIANT SPONGE

The structure of the universe is a bit like the structure of a natural sponge, with large empty spaces surrounded by walls or "filaments."

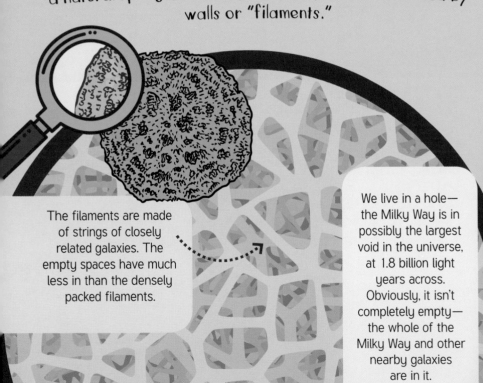

The filaments are made of strings of closely related galaxies. The empty spaces have much less in than the densely packed filaments.

We live in a hole—the Milky Way is in possibly the largest void in the universe, at 1.8 billion light years across. Obviously, it isn't completely empty—the whole of the Milky Way and other nearby galaxies are in it.

The universe is at least 93 billion light years across

That's how far we can measure —but it could be a lot bigger.

The edge of the visible universe is 46.5 billion light years away. That should mean the light left it 46.5 billion years ago, but that's not possible as the universe is only 13.8 billion years old.

Because space is expanding, more space is being added all the time between us and the most distant objects. So the light had already come some way toward us when the object was pushed further back.

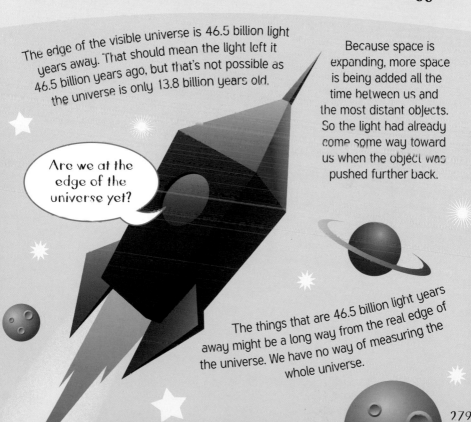

Are we at the edge of the universe yet?

The things that are 46.5 billion light years away might be a long way from the real edge of the universe. We have no way of measuring the whole universe.

GALAXIES ARE REALLY SPACED OUT

Andromeda is the galaxy nearest to ours, but it's not very near at all—it's 2,500,000 light years away.

As the Milky Way is 100,000 light years across, and Andromeda is 140,000 light years across, there's room for lots of empty space in between.

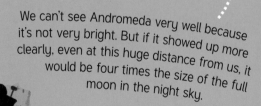

We can't see Andromeda very well because it's not very bright. But if it showed up more clearly, even at this huge distance from us, it would be four times the size of the full moon in the night sky.

THERE COULD BE TEN TIMES AS MANY LAZY BLACK HOLES AS WORKING ONES

We spot black holes by seeing matter go around them or spotting the signs of matter going toward them. But if a black hole has cleared out its local area already, there's nothing to see.

Scientists think there might be up to ten times as many black holes as we know about, just because they're sitting there doing nothing.

Lazy black holes will eventually go away. They very slowly leak radiation until they evaporate to nothing. But it takes a long time.

A black hole the mass of the Sun would take 10^{67} years (that's 1 followed by 67 zeroes) to disappear.

I'm not lazy! I've finished all my work!

PEOPLE FIRST SAW THE PLANETS AS DISKS IN 1608

Until the telescope was invented, no one could see that the planets are worlds rather than spots of light.

The idea that ours might not be the only world was revolutionary. Italian philosopher Giordano Bruno was burned at the stake in 1600 for (among other radical new ideas) suggesting there could be other worlds with other beings.

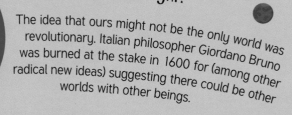

Before the telescope, the way the planets move, and don't twinkle, showed they're not the same as the stars. But that's all anyone knew.

Even in 1608, telescopes weren't powerful enough to show what the five visible planets were like—that three are rocky and two are made of gas.

THERE MIGHT BE AN UNCOUNTABLE NUMBER OF UNIVERSES

Some scientists suspect we're part of a multiverse—an infinite number of universes that branch off all the time.

This means all possibilities become real. There's a universe in which you had toast for breakfast and one in which you didn't.

There's a universe in which Earth is dominated by three-eyed blue creatures and many in which Earth doesn't even exist.

Our universe is just one in a bubbling pot of many, many universes.

IN THEORY, WE COULD TRAP ALL THE SUN'S ENERGY

A Dyson sphere is an imaginary mechanism for trapping all the energy from the Sun to use on Earth.

Never mind that we don't actually need anywhere near that much energy, science likes a challenge.

The sphere would wrap the Sun with solar panels to catch the energy it produces. None would escape into space.

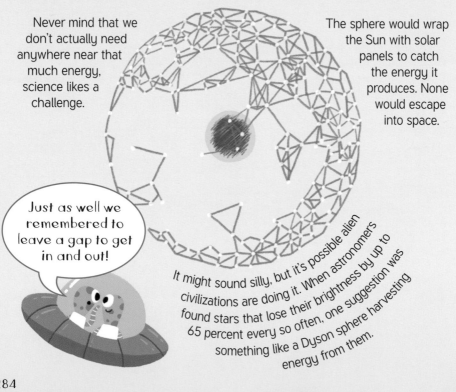

Just as well we remembered to leave a gap to get in and out!

It might sound silly, but it's possible alien civilizations are doing it. When astronomers found stars that lose their brightness by up to 65 percent every so often, one suggestion was something like a Dyson sphere harvesting energy from them.

There's a scale to rate how smart alien civilizations are

... even though we haven't found any yet. No harm in being prepared! The Kardashev scale gives six levels of technological progress for alien worlds, 0–5.

We don't even rate 1 on the scale—we have a level-0 civilization because we don't all cooperate (have a global society) and we don't use all the solar energy that falls on our planet.

A type-2 civilization can control its star and take all its energy.

A type-3 civilization could travel across their galaxy.

A type-4 civilization could control the energy of the entire universe.

And type-5 would be like gods, able to do anything at all.

IF WE HEAR FROM ALIENS, THEY WILL PROBABLY ALREADY BE DEAD

If we find a radio signal from aliens, it will have crossed space at the speed of light.

So if the aliens are 1,000 light years away, they will have sent their signal 1,000 years ago. Unless aliens live a very long time, those who sent it will probably be long dead—and they certainly will be before our reply reaches them in another 1,000 years.

We might get their messages after an entire civilization has died out. If the message takes 200,000 years to get to us, that's as long as modern humans have been around. Will we still be here in 200,000 years?

SOME PLANETS ARE HOMELESS

Rogue or wandering planets don't orbit a star, they just wander through space.

Some might have formed as part of a solar system and then been kicked out to fend for themselves. Others might have formed as solo planets.

Did your solar system kick you out too?

They're hard to spot, so we don't know how many there are but it's a lot. The lowest estimate is one for every four stars in the solar system, which could be 25–100 billion. The highest estimate is 100,000 times as many rogue planets as stars in the Milky Way.

The first pulsar was named LGM for "LITTLE GREEN MEN"

A pulsar is a rapidly rotating neutron star, left behind after the death of a star 20 times the mass of the Sun.

A research student called Jocelyn Bell found the first pulsar in 1967. She discovered regular radio pulses that repeated every 1.34 seconds. It seemed too regular to be natural, so was named "LGM" in case it was an alien radio signal.

It works a bit like a lighthouse, sending out a beam of radiation every time it goes around.

Some pulsars spin faster than the blades in a food processor, at hundreds of times a second.

A LIGHT YEAR ISN'T THE BIGGEST MEASUREMENT THERE IS

When we want to measure the size of galaxies, even light years aren't big enough. Galaxies are millions or billions of light years across.

The biggest unit astronomers can use is the gigaparsec—which is a billion parsecs. A parsec is 3.262 light years, or about 31 trillion km (19 trillion miles). Earth is 14 gigaparsecs from the edge of the observable universe.

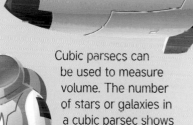

Cubic parsecs can be used to measure volume. The number of stars or galaxies in a cubic parsec shows the density of matter in space.

It's just a few parsecs to Grandma's house!

The Sun is the only star in its cubic parsec. But in globular clusters of stars there can be 100–1,000 stars in a cubic parsec.

SOMETIMES, ONE STAR SWALLOWS ANOTHER WHOLE

A rare kind of star called a Thorne—Zytkow object is a red supergiant with a working neutron star inside it.

Both might be formed in a supernova, but the neutron star is absorbed by the much larger supergiant.

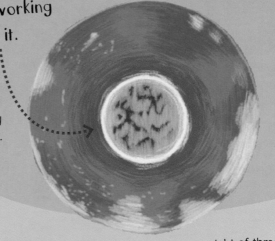

Sometimes, two neutron stars merge with each other. When they do, they make heavy metals.

Two neutron stars with the combined weight of three Suns merged in 2017, producing 3 to 13 times the mass of the Earth in solid gold!

We might just possibly have
HEARD FROM ALIENS ONCE

The "Wow! signal" arrived in 1977.

Everything about the signal is odd, leading astronomers to wonder if it was sent by aliens.

It's called the "Wow! signal" because the astronomer who spotted it wrote "Wow!" on the printout.

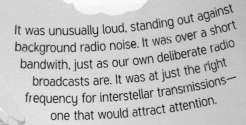

It was unusually loud, standing out against background radio noise. It was over a short bandwith, just as our own deliberate radio broadcasts are. It was at just the right frequency for interstellar transmissions— one that would attract attention.

It went on for 72 seconds and was never found again. It's still unexplained, more than 40 years later.

THE HUBBLE SPACE TELESCOPE

Hubble was the first telescope sited in space, launched on the Space Shuttle Discovery in 1990.

It travels at 8 km (5 miles) per second. It could travel across the USA in 10 minutes.

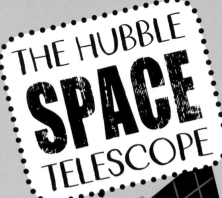

The first suggestion for a space telescope was made in 1923, before the first rocket had been launched.

Hubble orbits 547 km (340 miles) above Earth, going around the world every 97 minutes.

Hubble is serviced and repaired in space by astronauts on spacewalks.

Hubble has produced hundreds of thousands of images of space objects. It sends 120 gigabytes of data back to Earth every week.

Any astronomer in the world can apply for a slot of Hubble's time to look at whatever they want.

The most distant galaxy spotted by Hubble is 13.8 billion light years away.

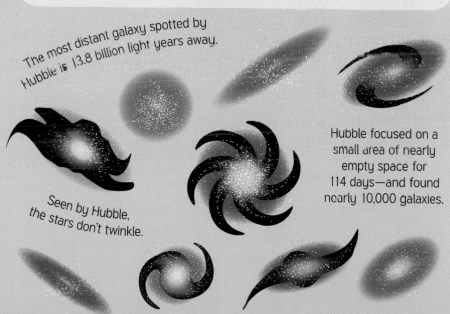

Seen by Hubble, the stars don't twinkle.

Hubble focused on a small area of nearly empty space for 114 days—and found nearly 10,000 galaxies.

There are many more stars in the universe than GRAINS OF SAND ON EARTH

Our galaxy probably has around 400 billion stars.

There are probably between 100 billion and a trillion galaxies. If they were all a similar size, there would be at least 400 billion x 100 billion stars, which is 20 sextillion (20,000,000,000,000,000,000,000) stars.

Researchers in Hawaii worked out the area and depth of all the world's beaches and the volume of a grain of sand. Then they calculated that there are 7.5 quintillion (7,500,000,000,000,000,000) grains of sand on Earth.

So there are more than 2,500 times as many stars as there are grains of sand.

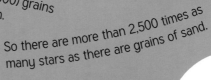

HUBBLE WENT WRONG
IMMEDIATELY

As soon as the Hubble telescope was in space, a fault in the mirror showed up.

It was uneven —but only by one fiftieth of the thickness of a sheet of paper. Even that was enough to make the images blurry and poor, no better than could have been gained from Earth.

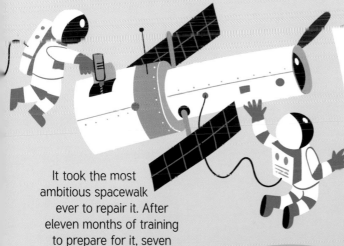

HUBBLE TELESCOPE

Instruction Manual

It took the most ambitious spacewalk ever to repair it. After eleven months of training to prepare for it, seven astronauts flew into space.

With five days of space walks and repairs, Hubble was fixed and—three years after launch—finally produced stunning images.

CHINA'S MEGATELESCOPE IS UNDER THREAT FROM TOURISTS WITH PHONES

The largest radio telescope with a single dish is in China; it's 500 m (1,650 ft) across.

But tourists using cell phones near radio telescopes disrupt the work it does and can make the telescopes useless.

There's a 5-km (3-mile) zone around the telescope where people aren't allowed to use their phones, but it's hard to enforce.

Bigger radio telescopes are made by linking antenna in widely spaced dishes. They're called array telescopes. The biggest is ALMA in Atacama, Chile. It has 66 dishes that can be spread over 16 km (10 miles).

WE DON'T KNOW WHAT MOST OF THE UNIVERSE IS

Adding up all the bits we know about, we can account for only one twentieth of the total mass of the universe.

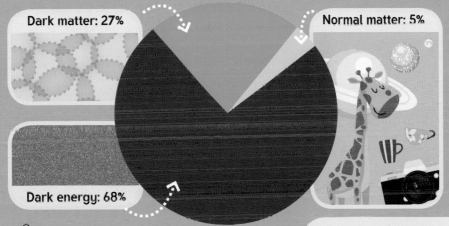

Dark matter: 27%

Normal matter: 5%

Dark energy: 68%

Only one twentieth of the universe is made of the normal matter we see in our bodies, other objects, and planets like Earth. Ninety-five percent is unknown.

The rest is made of dark energy (68 percent) and dark matter (27 percent). No one really knows what they are.

Dark matter could be lots of brown dwarfs or patches of dense matter that don't emit light. Or it could be a type of matter we have never met.

Andromeda is the only galaxy moving toward us

Andromeda is the closest galaxy to the Milky Way.

It's close enough that the gravity of both galaxies acts to pull them together (and they're going to crash—see page 245). All other large galaxies are too far from the Milky Way for gravity to pull them closer. The expansion of the universe pushes them further apart.

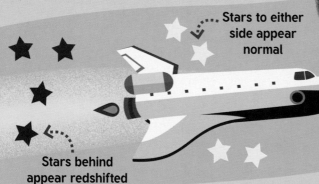

Stars to either side appear normal

Stars in front appear blueshifted

Stars behind appear redshifted

As galaxies or stars move away from us, the frequency of the light they throw out changes so that they look redder (called redshift).

It happens as expanding space stretches the wavelength of the light. Things moving toward us look bluish (called blueshifted).

EMPTY SPACE ISN'T EMPTY

There are lots of tiny energy particles in the empty space between stars and galaxies.

There are also a few particles of normal matter—about 1 atom of hydrogen in every cubic cm (16 atoms in every cubic in).

Dark matter

Dark energy

Normal matter

Empty space is also full of dark energy. It springs from nowhere, pushing matter further and further apart, and making the universe larger from within. But no one understands it or exactly how it works.

WE'VE BEEN SEARCHING FOR INTELLIGENT ALIENS SINCE 1984

The Search for Extra Terrestrial Intelligence (SETI) uses radio telescopes to look for evidence of aliens.

It will only find aliens advanced enough to have their own technology sending out radio signals.

Radio signals are our best hope of finding intelligent aliens, as we can't see conditions on distant planets.

Astronomers have a few ideas why we haven't heard from aliens:

We're too early—the first civilization to develop radio and space travel.

They're waiting for us to get more advanced before they get in touch.

We're being impatient— we just haven't looked long enough yet to find them.

They've learned contact is dangerous, so they're staying quiet or hiding.

Earth's leaked radio signals have only reached 100 light years so far—aliens might be further away.

We're too late—other civilizations have been and gone.

INDEX